1-2-3 CLARITY!

BANISH YOUR BLOCKS, DOUBTS, FEARS, AND LIMITING BELIEFS LIKE A SPIRITUAL BADASS

AMY SCOTT GRANT, MBA

SPIRITUAL ASS KICKER

Liberto
PRESS

Castle Rock, CO

Published by Liberto Press

Castle Rock, Colorado, USA

Cover design by Nick Zelinger, NZ Graphics

Book design and production by LibertoPress.com

Editing by Deb McLeod of DebMcLeod.com

Author photograph by Andrew E. Grant

Library of Congress Catalog Number: 2014921498

ISBN: 978-0-9862269-0-8

First Liberto Press printing, November 2014

ACKNOWLEDGEMENTS

To my husband and my children, the shimmery lights of my life.
You are a bunch of monkeys and I love you all so very much.

To my friend/editor/writing compadre Deb, you cannot begin
to know how much you have helped me.
But don't worry; I'll still let you buy me lunch.

To Paul, Rich, Great Aunt Theresa, Hammesh,
and my entire energy team, who rock more than anyone
(except them) could know.

CONTENTS

WHY READ THIS BOOK?

If I didn't know how the Universe really works, I'd be flattered that you chose *this* book.

But let's face it. You didn't arrive here by accident, and you and I both know it. By the time you're done reading, you'll understand why it *had* to be this book, and why it had to be *now*.

In the meantime, here's some data for your left-brain to munch on. I'm a master intuitive healer, Spiritual Ass Kicker, hilar-voyant (hilarious+clairvoyant), irreverently entertaining speaker, two-time bestselling author, and badass thought leader. I have cleared millions of blocks for thousands of people across twenty-nine countries. I have created dozens of powerful programs and premium courses and I get jaw-dropping results for teachers, accountants, sales people, entrepreneurs, moms, executives, coaches, artists, analysts, healers, and others just like you.

My full bio (including a sneak peek at my next holy-smokes project that's coming your way) is in the *About the Author* section at the end of this e-book.

But enough about me, let's talk about you. Are you ready to learn how to clear your biggest blocks, doubts, fears, and limiting beliefs? Hang onto your socks, because here we go.

Amy Scott Grant

INTRODUCTION

Never begin a book with a quote.

~Amy Scott Grant

What is a Spiritual Ass Kicker and more importantly, why would you want one?

You might be wondering what constitutes a Spiritual Ass Kicker, or what qualifies a person as such. I got a lot of pushback when I first started using that title, but I knew it fit because nothing else came close to describing what I do for people. No, I won't beat you up (physically or emotionally), and I don't push you around or get in your face. But I'm a straight shooter who kicks ass at identifying and permanently dissolving your core problems. I also have an offbeat, quick-witted, and often irreverent sense of humor, so consider yourself forewarned.

Breaking the Mold

According to bestselling author and thought leader Malcolm Gladwell, becoming masterful at something takes at least ten thousand hours of deliberate practice. That equates to roughly five years of full-time laser focus, pushing the limits of what you think you can do in order to expand and improve. I've been working full time as an intuitive healer since 2005, with a number of years of part-time study and personal application prior to that. It is these

1

years of intense focus and commitment to excellence that have helped me to become unequivocally *masterful* at healing and energy work.

The trouble is, when you hear phrases like "intuitive healer" or "energy worker," you tend to get a certain image in mind. I do not fit that image.

I do not wear Birkenstocks. I do not dress in long, flowing fabric. I do not smell of patchouli.

What about you? Are you more of a corporate type, a hippie, or perhaps one who dances to the beat of his/her own drum? Or perhaps you are only just discovering this vast and sometimes overwhelming playground of energy. Wherever you are is perfect, but I wonder if what you project to the world matches how you experience life on the inside?

Several years ago, I hired a friend of mine (I call her "Flach") for a long-overdue image makeover. By the time I'd had my second kid, I'd fallen into mommyhood—sure, I was still working and kicking ass at it, but I didn't look like I felt. I mostly wore jeans and golf shirts. And not in a hip, ironic way, but more along the lines of, "now that I have kids, my appearance is no longer a priority so I throw on any old thing." If you're a parent, you can probably relate to this. Flach arrived at my home and looked me up and down. She asked me what I wanted most as a result of our time together. I had already considered this (yes, I actually do practice what I preach. Clarity is my bestie) and I told her, "I want my outsides to match my insides."

Flach nodded, thinking. "The last time I saw you, we were in high school. You were kind of a badass then. Nothing crazy or stupid, but...a little edgy, a little outside-the-lines. Is that how you are today?"

I looked down at my drab clothing and then back at Flach. "Yeah. On the inside, anyway. I don't know what the hell happened to my 'look.'"

Flach is amazing. Throughout the whole weekend, even as she was editing my closet down to what felt like next to nothing, I never felt crappy because she didn't judge me for the choices I had made about my looks. If you're thinking, "Well, why would she?" then you've probably never met people in the fashion and makeover industry. They can be ruthless, cold, snotty, and insensitive.

But not Flach. She shrugged and said, "You had kids. Your priorities changed. Now you're settled in and ready to turn the attention back on you a bit. This is your time. It's your turn."

And right then, I relaxed. Everything would be okay now, I could feel it.

Now it's your turn. Whatever has happened in your life up until now is fine. Wherever you are right now is perfect. I'm going to walk you through this energy stuff, step by step, without judgment or prejudice. This is your time. It's your turn.

When I hired Flach, I was the Spiritual Ass Kicker everywhere in my life...except the way I looked. And like it or not, people do judge a book by its cover. You and I do it, too, whether we want to or not. We can't help it; it's how we're built as humans. If you don't believe me, buy a hideous shirt and wear it in public for a whole day. Notice how it changes the way you feel when you interact with people, and notice how people treat you. What you outwardly project to the world makes a difference in how you feel about moving through the world. The more clearing work you do, the more your appearance will begin to change and believe it or not, you will actually get better looking.

This is partly because you can remove decades of stress and strain from your face by clearing the stuff that's actually causing the distress, but there's more to it than that. The more you love yourself, the better you treat yourself. This means better choices in clothing and accessories, and improved self-care and grooming.

If this all sounds superficial to you, then you may be worse off than you thought. Just consider these two questions:

1. When you are out in public, would you prefer to interact with someone who has a nice appearance, is clean and well groomed and looks "put-together," or are you drawn to the

person who looks like they just rolled out of bed and threw on any old thing?

2. Do your outsides match your insides? In other words, does the appearance that you show to the outside world match your inner experience of life?

If you answered anything other than "hell yes!" to the second question, then there's room for growth, especially with regards to your self-love and acceptance. Clearing will help you with this. The more you clear, the more you will love yourself, and the less tolerant you will be for anything that's incongruent with a full and unapologetic expression of *you*.

Thanks to a couple of days with Flach, my outsides started to match my insides, and I felt like a million bucks. There is a sense of empowerment and confidence that comes with *congruency*. Authentically loving the way you look (or your career, or your relationship, or your bank account) means you can walk through life with total congruency because you are unabashedly you, no matter where, when, or with whom. This is what it means to be free.

What about you, right now?

Are you free to be you, and to express yourself fully? Can you be yourself in any situation, without apology? If you're like most people, the answer is, "Um, not exactly." I'll bet you have at least one relationship or one area of your life where you have to dial it down (or up), and make some adjustments to the real you, for one reason or another. It sucks, right?

You might have noticed that it takes a lot of effort to resist something. (If you've ever roughhoused with a three-year-old, you know what I'm talking about. Dammit, they are strong!) But when it comes to resisting who you truly are, it also takes mental, spiritual, and emotional effort. It's exhausting. And once you stop doing it, you'll be amazed by how liberated you feel.

At first glance, this book appears to be about clarity. It is, in large part. But my goal for you, dear seeker, is not *just* clarity. It's liberation. Freedom to be. Anytime, anywhere, with anyone.

Freedom will change your life.

In this book, I will help you to gain clarity and set yourself free by inviting you to consider different perspectives, by engaging you in provocative exercises and challenges, and by entertaining you with stories, laughter, and shoot-'em-straight no-BS language. Because that's just how I roll.

And that, dear seeker, is what a Spiritual Ass Kicker does and why you need one. Now let's get started.

Amy Scott Grant

LAGNIAPPE: My Gift to You

In my hometown of New Orleans, we use the word "lagniappe" (pronounced "lan-yapp") to mean "a little something extra." Here's a little lagniappe for you.

Have you ever wished you could have an "easy button" for life?

Now you can! This powerful yet simple tool will assist you in making countless decisions and choices throughout your day, and you can rest easy knowing you're always making the most optimal decision on any matter in any given moment.

Plus, you can use this tool to discern whether someone is telling you truth or not. How many situations can you think of where *that* would come in handy?

Visit **www.InfoYesNo.com** to claim your free Truth Testing mini-course, a $97 value.

Amy Scott Grant

CHAPTER ONE
More than a Moment of Clarity

Never underestimate the power of clarity.

~Amy Scott Grant

Have you ever heard people tell you a story about their life, and right at the turning point they say, "And then I had a moment of clarity," and then everything changed?

Clarity appears to be a natural phenomenon of the mind, when the planets align and all the pieces come together and we have that singularly blessed "a-ha!" moment. Remember that scene in "Back to the Future" where Doc falls and bumps his head on the sink and then gets the idea for the flux capacitor? His moment of clarity shows up as a flash of genius.

But why are moments of clarity so few and far between? I expect it's because we don't spend nearly enough of our time thinking about anything of great importance. But maybe you're different. Let's find out with this quick exercise.

Exercise: Rewind

In your mind, rewind to two weeks ago today. Can you remember what preoccupied your thoughts then? Glance at your day planner if you need helping remembering what you were doing two weeks ago. Now fast forward through each day (again, use the schedule if it helps) and notice the predominant thoughts you had. If it's too hard to remember, you can read through your journal, skim the "sent" box of your email, and review your texts or Skype chats from two weeks ago. Something was on your mind, what was it?

Now (and this part is totally subjective) how important would you rate those predominant thoughts to be? Were you working on a cure for cancer? Solving the global food crisis? Figuring out a way to dissolve organized crime? Were you working on yourself, taking active steps to release your blocks, fears or doubts, or to improve yourself in some way? Were you mainly thinking of ways you can contribute, either to yourself, your family, your neighborhood, your job/career, your country or the world? Were these the predominant thoughts that ruled your mind and your life a couple of weeks ago, and again today?

Or were you in fact like most people in the world, worrying about money, mentally criticizing your body, fretting over your job/career, judging others, harboring grudges, being concerned about health of yourself or a loved one, regretting things you did or didn't say, things you did or didn't do, or resisting and stuffing emotions like anger, frustration, jealousy, greed, irritation, and so on?

Perhaps you were somewhere in-between. This exercise is not designed to make you feel bad or wrong for whatever you typically spend time thinking about. Rather, it's presented here as a way to make you think.

It's important to think about what you think about!

This is not a book on "positive thinking." However, I would challenge you to consider this: if your internal background conversation is often dominated by negative thoughts, you are likely feeling frustrated with all or part of your life. This may leave you feeling as though you're living in a fog.

But the fact that you're reading this book right now is a clear sign that at least part of you wants to get off the foggy ride and get yourself some clarity.

You don't have to wait for a moment of clarity to strike. You can *invoke* moments of clarity, like flashes of insight and strokes of genius. You have the power in your hands and your heart right now. And reading this book is a great first step in that direction.

I hold the intention that as you read this book, you receive moments of clarity and flashes of insight. It would be wise of you to write these down as they arrive. Clarity that isn't followed up with action tends to get a bit fuzzy in the memory banks, evaporating like wisps of smoke.

When clarity strikes, write it down.

That's a simple enough action for now, and capturing that clarity means you can always have it as a reference point; a touchstone to bring you back to center.

There are of course other ways to invoke clarity, and that is what we will cover in this book. I use a phrase often, called "getting clear."

What does it mean to get clear?

When I speak or teach people how to get *clear,* the meaning of the expression is twofold: having clarity, and being free from obstruction.

Clarity refers to an easy understanding of your truth. When you are faced with a decision and you have clarity, the choice is evident. When you find yourself in a sticky situation, you look for clarity or truth (what's really going on here?) before you make your next move. This understanding of what is true for you is what creates the "a-ha!" moment, with the optional nod of the head. (Did you nod just now?)

Releasing blocks, doubts, fears, and limiting beliefs is how you become free from obstruction. If you want to increase your income, but you have doubts about your ability to earn more, or you have fears about squandering money if you receive too much too fast, then you have a lot to gain by *clearing* these obstacles.

In working with me, you can expect me to remove obstructions such as doubts, fears, phobias, blocks, limiting beliefs, etc. Often when I perform a clearing at the energetic level, there are physical signs of evidence that follow, as experienced by my client Cassie:

A few hours after our clearing session, my right foot balanced itself! It was so exciting and I know your work is working! I've been working on healing that ankle/outer foot for years and it just fell into place yesterday.

What's so great about getting clear?

Can you remember a time when you were expected to do something, but you lacked the clear instructions or guidance as to how to do it? If you pressed onward despite your lack of clarity, and tried to complete the task anyway, what was your experience?

You may have felt frustrated, irritated, angry, confused, or overwhelmed. Not a pretty place to hang out in your mind.

Now in contrast, think back to your favorite teacher. What made him or her so special? I'll bet this person gave you clear direction, clear expectations, and praised you for work well done. Around this person, you may have felt uplifted, inspired, and successful. Yes, praise is always welcome, but it's *clarity* that makes tough tasks easier to tackle.

Likewise, it's clarity that creates a space for powerful breakthroughs, as Elaine experienced:

Never in my wildest dreams did I ever consider with all the information I gave you that you would be so extremely intuitive as to zero in on the dearest and most important needs in my life at that particular time AND in the order that I most needed to experience peace and healing.

You my dear have a 'gift' and used it most effectively to move me through the most positive and enlightening experience I have had in years. I had a friend 'gifted' as you are who passed away in 1997 and I have not found anyone who has come anywhere close to her 'gift' until you, Amy. From the very beginning session, I felt a deeper sense of peace, tranquility and lightness I have not felt in eons.

I feel like a new woman... with so many more expectations for a fuller, richer, more abundant life than ever before. I awaken

*each day with a greater feeling of appreciation for the release
from the burdens I had been carrying for so long.*

*With gratitude and appreciation for the 'gift' that you have and
are.*

When I was a kid, I was clear. I knew things, but I couldn't
explain how or why I knew them. I don't mean I was a smart-ass
(although I kind of was. Still am, actually.). I often knew unusual
or important or secret things, which surprised the adults in my life.
I remember going to my first Chinese restaurant at the age of five
or six. My family was floored to watch me use chopsticks with
ease, and when my mother asked me, "Where did you learn how to
use chopsticks?" I casually replied, "I don't know, I just picked it
up somewhere." The whole table burst out laughing, but I had no
idea why.

Eventually, I noticed the adults' sideways glances and nervous
laughter every time I joined "grown-up" conversations, and it
became evident that I was different. I soon realized that other
people were not as comfortable with my insights as I was, so I tried
to blame it on my imaginary friend, Chookel. (My brothers teased
me incessantly about the name, pronounced "chew-kull," but what
could I do? Sure, I would have liked "Jennifer" just fine, but when
she first showed up, she said "Hi, I'm Chookel" and that was that.)
But news of an imaginary friend who told secrets and taught me
interesting things wasn't well-received. Then, one day, after
receiving particularly disturbing feedback on one of my
"knowings," I shut down my intuition completely.

A funny thing happens when we deny our true nature, only it's
not funny at all. We suddenly feel lost, confused, and uncertain. By
the age of thirteen, I had made multiple suicide attempts,
convinced that I did not belong in this world. The idea of living life
without being truly known or understood by another human being
felt like too much for me to bear. I needed answers, and
desperately fast.

That's when my moment of clarity arrived. I attracted a book into my life, the perfect book for me at that moment in time (Norman Vincent Peale's *Power of Positive Thinking*).

Changing my thoughts got me over the hump, but positive thinking couldn't sustain me for long. I soon realized (in another moment of clarity) that it takes a tremendous amount of vigilance and willpower to police those pesky negative thoughts—especially when times are toughest.

It was hard, because I don't have a lot of willpower. (Sound familiar?) Which is why—in another moment of clarity—I realized it made more sense to shift my *beliefs* instead of trying to control my thoughts. After all, don't our most repetitive thoughts stem from our deep-seated beliefs? I figured if I could change the beliefs, the thoughts would naturally follow suit.

Unfortunately, most new thought teachers will try to convince you that the way to change your beliefs is with affirmations, which requires writing out a new thought statement, and repeating it ad nauseum. Yawn. While this method does work—eventually—it is exhausting. In search of a better way, I returned to my natural intuition and my own process of "knowing." It was through this process that I learned to swiftly and permanently shift beliefs, and sure enough, I was right! The corresponding thoughts followed naturally.

Clearing your blocks can only be described as "hot damn!" It is highly satisfying and borders on addictive. The resulting clarity brings a sense of freedom that cannot be compared to anything else. I immediately fell in love with the process and the results. Imagine your biggest stumbling block—the one that keeps you up at night, consumes your waking thoughts, and prevents you from achieving what you desire. Now, imagine it were gone *forever*. How would that feel? What could you do if you no longer had that block? What would now be possible for you?

That's right—anything becomes possible. Doors that were once closed now bust wide open and opportunities abound. I was so exhilarated by my own results, it felt like a natural transition to help other people do the same.

Sure, I resisted at first. I remember the first time I cleared for someone else. I was on the phone with a friend of mine who I hadn't known very long. He was a marketer who wasn't big on spiritual stuff, so I was especially nervous about mentioning my newfound skill. But he repeatedly complained about a headache, and every time he mentioned it, I got an intuitive hit that I could clear it. You can probably imagine what went through my head. What if I can't do it? What if he thinks I'm weird? What if he laughs at me?

Spoiler alert: it did work. His headache disappeared! He was amazed and grateful and my perspective began to shift. I realized if I could heal someone else (a non-believer, no less), then certainly there were a lot of people I could help. With more practice, I realized I had a knack for clearing work, so I turned *clearing* into my profession. Over the years, I have cleared millions of limiting beliefs for thousands of individuals, subsequently empowering them to become far more successful in life, in love, and in business.

I use my true nature (my intuition) to go to the root and figure out why you created the belief in the first place, and what we need to do to shift it. This shift, or complete release of the old belief, is what I call "clearing," because we *clear* the underlying cause of your stagnation/self-sabotage/lack of results. In a *clearing,* we get rid of the beliefs that don't serve you, and sometimes we replace them with new beliefs, designed to support the achievement of your goals.

Releasing limiting beliefs is a fast and powerful process, because as soon as the limiting beliefs are gone, your thoughts will naturally change. And when your thoughts change, your results change. And when your results change for the better—success!

The process all begins with *clarity.* You'll be happy to know that you don't have to wait for a moment of clarity to randomly strike like lightning. You can *invoke* clarity. The clearing process acts like a lightning rod, drawing clarity to you and helping you to create that oh-so-yummy pivotal shift.

Chap-Recap #1

At the end of each chapter, we'll recap the essential takeaway points and give you a simple plan of action to implement what you've just learned.

Food for Thought:

1. You don't have to wait for a moment of clarity or flash of genius to randomly strike. You can use the clearing methods in this book to *invoke* clarity.
2. It's important to think about what you think about.
3. When clarity strikes, write it down.
4. "Getting clear" means creating clarity and releasing obstacles in order to clear the path ahead.
5. Positive thinking and affirmations can only take you so far, but with clarity, tough tasks are easier to tackle, solutions become apparent, possibilities abound, and life gets better.
6. Clearing is a quick and powerful process, because as soon as the limiting beliefs are gone, your thoughts change, and then your results change. It all begins with clarity.

Action Plan:

1. If you don't already have a journal or notebook, get one. Begin writing down your insights and moments of clarity, and use the notebook to complete the remaining exercises in this book.
2. Practice Praxis (because who can resist such good tongue-twisting word play?): The Power of Intention

EXERCISE: The Power of Intention

I've taught and practiced feng shui (the art of arranging spaces for maximum energy flow) for several years. It's an ancient and complex process that I like to break down into small, manageable steps and practical applications. To me, the most fascinating thing about feng shui is how quickly we can make dramatic changes in our lives, simply by moving stuff around in our home or office, and doing so with *intention*.

Intention simply means "an aim or purpose." The more you incorporate intention into everything you do, the more purposefully you will live, and the more rich and fulfilling your life will become. I could probably write an entire book on that topic (and perhaps I shall), but for now, let's practice using intention in a way that matters.

Take a minute now to imagine you have arrived at a point in the future when you are clear and focused. There is no confusion in your mind or your life. You know your next move. Choices and decisions come easily, and you feel relaxed and peaceful. What do you notice that's different? Have your relationships changed? Has your occupation changed? Any shift in your financial circumstances? What about your body? Is it different? How do you feel emotionally? Name the specific emotions that arise.

Take a few minutes now to jot down this experience and record your observations.

When you have finished, write down the following in your own handwriting:

The ways and the paths are becoming clear.
Clarity is mine now.
I am clear.
I am clear.
I am clear.

Amy Scott Grant

CHAPTER TWO

What's the Cost?

If it ain't congruent, don't do it.

~Amy Scott Grant

Over the years, I've noticed that many of my clients use the phrase "part of me." For example:

"Part of me feels like I should leave him, but part of me still loves him."

"Part of me is worried about money, but another part of me knows that's only making things worse financially."

"Part of me wants to stay at my job, but then there's a part of me that wants to just walk away and do something else entirely."

"Part of me is happy for her, but part of me is jealous and says it's unfair."

Can you relate to this? Many times, we feel internally divided about an issue or circumstance, or a decision. This internal conflict creates confusion, which can lead to frustration, overwhelm or despair.

Does *all* of you ever want the same thing?

This is a simple concept called congruency. Congruency means "agreement." When all of you is in agreement, there is no internal conflict and the result is congruency. Thanks to my image makeover from Flach, my appearance is now congruent with the rest of me.

But what happens when something is incongruent?

- ➢ You wind up giving away services you should be charging for
- ➢ You let people take advantage of you
- ➢ You stay in relationships longer than you should
- ➢ You get roped into stuff you don't really want
- ➢ You get stuck in a payment agreement, a contract, or a partnership that isn't working
- ➢ You wind up broke, sick, or depressed

The bottom line is, when you agree to something that's incongruent, you will soon feel bitter, frustrated, and trapped. You may think you're mad at the person who "talked you into it" but in reality, you're mad at yourself for making a choice that some part of you knew was incongruent, but that you allowed yourself to make anyway. Yeah, it sucks.

Why do people make incongruent choices?

It happens all the time and for a variety of reasons. Think of some area of your life where you feel as though you're stuck with a commitment you made, which you wish you hadn't made, or that you could easily escape from. Have you got one? Okay, good. Now think back to the moment when you first said "yes" to it. Which of the following reasons applies to that circumstance:

- ➢ You wanted to look good (ego)
- ➢ You wanted to save face/avoid looking bad (ego)
- ➢ You felt bad for the other person and to try to offset that, you agreed to help (fixing vs. feeling)
- ➢ You couldn't help yourself (addiction)

> ➢ You said yes without thinking (yes-itis)
> ➢ You were avoiding something else (resistance)
> ➢ You owed them a favor, or multiple favors (guilt)
> ➢ You allowed yourself to be manipulated (low level of self-love)
> ➢ The expectations were unclear (lack of clarity)

Perhaps you are thinking that none of these reasons apply and that you said yes for some other, more noble reason. But before you hop back on that high horse, take a moment to re-read the first two, as the vast majority of our motivations fall under these categories. If you really had a noble reason for wanting to help (for example, "my heart went out to him and I just wanted to help in some way"), then the odds are very unlikely that you would *today* feel stuck or trapped with that decision, unless something from the list above is causing you to continue when it would actually be congruent to walk away.

Clarity is the first step to congruency, and congruency is the prerequisite to freedom.

All I can say is that you are a woman of your word (which I already knew). I didn't think I had started very far down my new path and BAM! I would say that miracles have started happening so thank you for everything tonight and thank you for giving me that little push. It's greatly appreciated.

It's hard to describe, but last night around supper, I really did start to feel like I was getting my power back. When you have given your power to someone for 15 years, it's a very amazing experience to have it come back. Kind of like slaying the dragons or something...

~ Martha H., New York

Here's what's available to you when you bring more clarity into your life:

> You get in tune with yourself and discover your most reliable method for making decisions and choices.
> You make decisions and choices only when you are clear.
> You ask questions when anything is unclear.
> You continue asking questions until you have perfect clarity.
> You may ask for more time. ("Let me sleep on it and give you an answer tomorrow.")
> You self-advocate. You understand you are not a doormat. Because of this, others treat you with respect and consideration.
> You are aware enough to realize when a commitment has devolved from its original intention, and you make a clear choice whether to readdress it and make it work, or walk away.
> If you choose to walk away, it is because doing so is completely congruent. Therefore, you are clear in your communication with the other parties and you are unaffected by their emotions, tantrums, or temporary frustrations.
> You experience less drama, and have less tolerance for the drama of others.
> You attract exquisite friends, mentors, partners, clients, customers, neighbors, acquaintances, and even "chance encounters."
> You are more productive.
> You know what you want.
> You are able to ask for what you want and what you need.
> You easily set goals and achieve them.
> You are in the driver's seat.
> You are calmer, more peaceful, more focused, and more relaxed.
> Your life rocks.

You may have noticed that when individuals become very successful, they actually get better looking. I used to think it was because they had more money, so they could afford a stylist, or more expensive clothing, makeup, shoes, and accessories. But that's not what's at the heart of it.

When you create more success in your life, and when you do it in a way that is congruent with who you are, you dramatically decrease your stress level.

The first place we see evidence of stress is on the face. Scientific research has proven that the visible signs of aging are caused not by the passage of time, but by the accumulation of stress. This includes environmental stress such as UV exposure, smoking and second-hand smoke, exposure to toxins, etc.

When you are congruent, your stress levels drop and it shows on your face. Try this for yourself and see. Live a life of congruency and clarity day by day and soon people will start making comments like, "You look different," and "Have you lost weight?"

[The] calls have been creating some awesome results. Not only did I win a ticket to the event, I have some investments and just received my month end statement and the investments did much better than they have for a long time, they made double what I thought they would. Went out to grab a bite to eat last night with some friends. There was a draw at the pub to have your bill covered. I won!!! The amazing thing about this is that historically I did not win. There could have been 2 names in a hat and I would not win.

Obviously this is changing. SOOOOOO COOOOL. THANK YOU!

~Shannon P., Calgary, Alberta

The people I've worked with run the gamut and span the globe. I have cleared blocks for working professionals with high-profile jobs, as well as entrepreneurs, healers, coaches, celebrities, marketers, teachers, artists, government analysts, engineers, stay-at-home moms, and more. Most people find me when they've tried other stuff, but they haven't gotten the results they wanted. They set an intention for a mentor, or they go looking for one. Many are bored with run-of-the-mill coaches or they may feel disenchanted with healers who don't produce tangible results. But I succeed where others fail. People seek me out because I am masterful, and I am honest.

I'm a bit unorthodox in that I will tell you if I can't help you. If it's not a fit for us to work together, I don't mind telling you so, and in a way that is straightforward yet kind. In many cases, I will refer you to someone else who I know can help you.

Why would I do that? You might be thinking I'm foolish for turning down business and clients.

But if it ain't congruent, I don't do it.

I've learned this from that cruel and wicked teacher, "experience." Years ago I took on a client who was not a good fit. I didn't know about Calamity Jane's long psychiatric history when I agreed to work with her, but even from the start, my gut was uneasy about enrolling her as a client. I ignored my gut because at that time, I was building a practice and I was focused on filling all the client slots. So like a hungry dog, I said "yes" to every bone the Universe tossed my way.

As it turned out, she was batshit crazy. I had to get my lawyer involved. Talk about incongruent! Even though she had told me she wanted her issues cleared, she did not want to hear anything I said if it contradicted her narrow view of herself and the world. In other words, she didn't want to hear the truth. She shut down, and was massively resistant. Working with her cost me time, mental strain, emotional distress, and huge amounts of agitation. Most of all, I was frustrated that I couldn't reach her, that she wouldn't let me in. When she started harassing me by sending me threatening emails, I had to involve my attorney and we ultimately terminated the relationship. Epic fail.

It was a nightmare for both of us, but the lesson I learned from it was powerful and lasting: if it ain't congruent, don't do it.

If you're still not convinced that it pays to make only congruent choices, consider what the actual cost is to you. Besides everything you're giving up (freedom, peace of mind, happiness, and ease), look at the additional burdens you're taking on:

> Worry, which causes you stress and shows on your face
> The actual monetary costs involved—penalties, fees, lost income, interest, etc.
> Anxiety that can keep you awake at night (loss of sleep leads to decreased productivity and diminished personal energy, which means quality of life suffers)
> The list goes on and on, but I think you get the point

Hopefully by now, you can forgive my transgression from proper grammar and shout it out loud with me:

If it ain't congruent, don't do it!

Next we'll ease into the actual clearing process, which has three steps:

Step 1: Identify the core issue.

Step 2: Clear the underlying block.

Step 3: Verify it's completely cleared, then rinse and repeat.

Naturally, there's more to it, otherwise I would have offered you a tri-fold pamphlet instead of a whole book. In the next few chapters, we'll look at each of these steps in greater detail.

Chap-Recap #2

Food for Thought:

1. When all of you is in agreement, there is no internal conflict, and the result is congruency.
2. When you agree to something that's incongruent, you will soon feel bitter, frustrated, and trapped.
3. Most incongruent choices are made to either make yourself look good or to avoid looking bad.
4. Clarity is the first step to congruency, and congruency is the prerequisite to freedom.
5. When you create more success in your life, and when you do it in a way that is congruent with who you are, you dramatically decrease your stress level.

Action Plan:

Take some time to write down your answers to the following questions.

Where in your life do you feel trapped in a commitment?

What other feelings do you have about the situation?

Think back to the time when you made the commitment. What was your internal motivator at that time (refer back to the list if necessary)?

Practice Praxis: Reclaiming Control

What do you fear might happen if you were to break the commitment?

What is the most likely outcome if you break this commitment?

What is the most likely outcome if you don't break the commitment?

What would be the most congruent thing to do right now?

What would be the ideal outcome if anything were possible?

What one tiny step could you take today that would begin to bring the situation back into congruency for you?

Now take that step, and write about what actually happened.

Amy Scott Grant

CHAPTER THREE

Step 1. Identify the Core Issue

Your best bet is to find the root cause and clear it. Otherwise, you're on a never-ending wild goose chase.

~Amy Scott Grant

Identify the core issue. When you're working on yourself, this is sometimes easier said than done. In a later chapter, we'll get into resistance and what happens when you sabotage your own clearing efforts. But for now, let's just look at just three of the ways you can dig deep and uncover that core issue.

The core issue, which I sometimes refer to as the "originating incident," is the moment at which you made a decision or choice, adopted a belief, or created an agreement that is still with you today. At the time that you made that choice or took on that belief, you did so as a coping mechanism. It served you at the time, but now it's a hindrance and you want to let it go.

This is the key that sets my work apart from many other healers in my industry: by resolving the originating incident, the clearing becomes permanent. If you don't go *all* the way back to the place where you first took on the belief, you will see no results, or at best, only temporary results. My unique gift is the ability to swiftly and easily locate that originating incident, so that the issue can be permanently resolved; hence my use of the word "cleared." When a check clears your account, the money is gone. It's *cleared.*

29

Except of course this is better, because unlike money, what's gone is something you don't want or need any more.

Think of it this way. Do you have any huge weeds that grow where you live? Here in Colorado, we have dandelions. Not the cute little yellow flowers or the white puff balls that you can use to make a wish and blow. Our dandelions can grow taller than me, with stalks the diameter of my wrist! (And it's a big-boned wrist, at that!) It takes a lot more than a weed whacker to get rid of these suckers. One way to rid your yard of unsightly weeds is to cut them down. But what happens then? They grow back, usually faster than the grass. The problem returns, worse than ever.

What if you pulled up the weeds? You certainly could. It's more effective than mowing, although it takes longer and requires more physical effort. Your shoulders and back may be aching the next day. Plus, there's always the chance that you miss some of the root, or it breaks off below the surface. If so, you can bet it'll grow back soon enough, and then you're back at square one.

But what if you used a toxic weed killer spray to destroy the root? You would walk around your property and spray all the weeds at ground level, and within a day or two, they would shrivel up and fall, at which point you can easily gather up the remnants.

My clearing methods are better than weed killer because when we clear something, it doesn't destroy all your nearby grass and flowers! Clearing with me pinpoints only the root of what you don't want, and completely clears that space. Plus it doesn't leave a dead, ugly mess—instead it completely dissolves the entire block, so there's nothing left and nothing to clean up. Ah, if only my kitchen were this sophisticated.

Once the space is cleared of your block or fear or limiting belief, what could you plant in that fertile soil instead?

Anything you wanted! Hopes, dreams, and new ways of being. The possibilities are endless once you clear the blocks. See? I told you this was exciting. Let's remember the main point here:

It is *essential* that you go back to the originating incident and resolve it, otherwise the blocks will resurface.

Here are three of my easiest methods for finding the root cause or the originating incident.

Method #1: Pick a Pattern

We all have destructive patterns. Even the most "together" of people have their weaknesses. Surely you know at least one thin, beautiful, successful woman who always dates the wrong guy. Maybe you've met the spiritual leader with the addiction to chocolate (or soda, or candy, or cigarettes), or the average man whose life works well—except that he turns into the Hulk and flips out if anyone questions his integrity.

When you're the one repeating the pattern, it can be hard to spot, at least until you become ready to shift it. And heaven help the friend or counselor who points it out to you with irrefutable evidence *before* you are ready to release it! Your inner Hulk will surely devour that poor soul.

Here are some examples of negative patterns. Yours may be completely different, and you may be in denial about admitting you actually have any of these, but by the time you've finished reading this list, you will hopefully have identified at least one pattern that you'd like to remove from your life.

Examples of destructive patterns include:

> Getting angry or irritated at a certain person, regardless of what they say or do
> Beating yourself up mentally or emotionally with negative internal self-talk
> Criticizing yourself for the same thing over and over
> Addiction to a substance or activity (chocolate, crunchy/salty items, dairy/creamy foods, sugar, soda, caffeine, tobacco, pot, coffee, alcohol, sex, narcotics, work, sleeping, video games, prescription drugs, etc.)
> Criticizing your body when you look in the mirror or at a photo of yourself

- Attracting friends/lovers/business partners who are not a good fit for you
- Overspending/spending money without thinking, buying things you can't afford right now, buying on credit
- Letting other people manipulate you
- Worrying about what other people think
- Biting your nails, chewing on your hair, grinding your teeth
- Speaking in a self-deprecating manner
- Refusing money (for example, you provide client services for free, you refuse to let a friend pay for lunch, you don't follow up with people who owe you money, and so on.)
- Nervous laughter
- Perfectionism
- Defending someone else, or your own choices, unnecessarily
- Talking in disclaimers ("I don't know why I'm telling you this, but…" or "This doesn't make any sense, but I…" or "This may sound dumb, but…")
- Putting your own needs last
- Apologizing constantly
- Saying yes to everything, even if it's not congruent or you don't want to
- Gossip
- Not buying things you want/need even though you have the money because you're worried about money running out
- Procrastination (more about that later, wink wink)

There are likely thousands of patterns like these, but right now, I'm inviting you to just choose one that you have, that you are now ready to face and release. This is the pattern you'll use as your practice clearing for the remainder of this book.

Being *ready* to release the block is essential. Years ago, I knew I was addicted to sugar, but I didn't want to do anything about it. I was afraid it would mean I'd have to give up sugar forever, and I just wasn't ready to do that. That one fear prevented me from being ready and willing to release my sugar addiction for nearly five years. But once I was ready, I made the decision to face the fear and the clearing happened in the blink of an eye. Now, years later, I can eat sweets if I want to, in moderate quantities, and without any trace of compulsion or dependency. (For which my kidneys and blood sugar levels must surely thank me.)

Not all negative patterns are addictions. Biting your nails is not an addiction, it's a nervous habit. Some negative patterns simply involve the use of language that doesn't create the kind of result that you want. Have you ever met a person who's constantly apologizing for everything? They sound a bit like this:

"Hi, Amy, it's Becky. I'm sorry to bug you but do you have a minute?"

"Sure, I was just about to start dinner."

"Oh, I'm sorry. I should have known it's dinnertime there. Never mind, you can just call me tomorrow. Sorry to bother you."

"It's not a problem, I've got a few minutes. What's up?"

"Well, I'm sorry to call you with something so trivial, but…"

Then I'll bet she apologizes again as part of her good-bye. "Sorry I held you up," or something to that effect.

How does it feel when you speak to someone like Becky? I don't know about you, but for me it's just draining. I would probably have rolled my eyes by the time I said, "It's not a problem." For starters, I value my time so if I've actually given someone my mobile number, I don't appreciate having to spend time assuring them that it was okay that they called me. It's irritating that it takes so long for the person to just get to the point of the conversation. People who apologize all the time come across as whiny, needy, depressing, and in some cases, pathetic. We may even find ourselves letting those calls go to voicemail, just so we don't have to hear the person verbally wringing their hands.

Over-apologizing is not an addiction, but it's definitely a destructive pattern. If you over-apologize, people will not take you seriously (even when there's a legitimate reason to apologize), and they won't get to see all the wonderful qualities that you have to offer. This is a pattern that is definitely worth shifting, if you're willing to release it.

Once you've identified the destructive pattern you'd like to tackle, the next step is to find the common denominator. What emotion, thought, fear, or limiting belief is always present when the pattern occurs?

In the example of Becky, our over-apologizer, what are some of the reasons she might habitually use the word "sorry"? Here are a just a few possible reasons:

From her childhood:

> ➢ Her parents may have believed children should be seen and not heard.
> ➢ She may have been over-disciplined for speaking up or interrupting.
> ➢ Perhaps one of her parents or influential adults was always apologizing, which means she learned to model their behavior.
> ➢ Her parents may have over-praised or over-emphasized apologies, or otherwise rewarded obedience while discouraging boldness and independence.

From her present:

> ➢ She may have an overbearing boss who doesn't value her worth as a person.
> ➢ She could be in an abusive relationship.
> ➢ She might have a spouse or partner who is overly critical of her.
> ➢ Perhaps she has very low self-esteem and truly believes she is inconveniencing anyone who takes the time to listen to her.

From a past life:

> ➤ Maybe she has a major regret she hasn't resolved, and now spends every day attempting to be "sorry enough" (i.e., stuck in a loop).
> ➤ She could have beliefs that she is a "sorry excuse for a person" or something equally detrimental to her self-worth, carried over from a prior lifetime.
> ➤ She may have lived a lifetime as a slave, a concubine, or some other experience where she was taught she was "less than" others.
> ➤ She might have been abused or experienced trauma that is unresolved and is now triggered by certain types of people or relationships in this lifetime.

By looking closely at the pattern itself, we can begin to discover its root cause. For example, if Becky the over-apologizer finds herself increasing her normal use of the word "sorry" around *men,* this would be worth noting, as it would indicate an originating incident that involved a male. We could then look back to Becky's childhood (father, brothers, uncles, male teachers, coaches, etc.) and if we come up short there, we would then delve into her past lives.

Alternatively, it could be the corresponding *feeling* that triggers the apologies. For example, she may feel insecure, or inadequate, or "less than" someone she perceives to be smarter, prettier, more talented, more important, more successful, etc.

In other cases, the pattern is related to a specific person (or anyone who reminds Becky of this person), a certain time of year, or a particular phase of a cycle. For examples, if she has issues with being a woman, she may find she is more sensitive than usual and apologizes more frequently during certain stages of her menstrual cycle. I have even seen situations where negative patterns manifested at a certain age.

I once worked with a client who was dreading turning twenty-seven. I know, right? It sounds hard to believe. We could understand someone dreading a milestone year like thirty, forty, fifty, or sixty-five, but age twenty-seven seems so random at first glance. Yet, as her twenty-seventh birthday approached, she grew more and more anxious about it, so she asked for my help. I discovered a past life trauma whereby she had died a horrible death at (for that era, the ripe old age of) twenty-seven, and this was triggering her anxiety in this lifetime.

I can remember as a kid I worried for months after my mother turned fifty-four because I knew her mother had died at age fifty-five. Subconsciously, I was worried that the same could happen to her. (Spoiler alert: It didn't. The woman is now in her eighties and still going strong.) With my client, we used step two (see next chapter) to go back to the originating incident and complete the past, and then her anxiety around turning twenty-seven completely disappeared. That's the beauty of clearing! But beware any healer who only wants to discuss your childhood or your current life's traumas because to do so would be to miss out on a vast source of your anxieties, fears and unmet expectations from those past life experiences.

Remember, you must find the *root* cause and dissolve it; otherwise the pattern will never really be gone.

If Becky discovers that she is subconsciously afraid of men, which is why she always apologizes for herself when she is around anyone of the male gender, she can clear it. But if she thinks it's because her last boyfriend was an abusive, narcissistic jerk, she could clear that, but it's not going to change anything going forward. Because think about it, *why* did she accept such a jackass of a boyfriend in the first place? Which brings us to the next method for identifying the root cause.

Method #2: Why5

The Why5 is a simple yet powerful method that helps you get to the root of something, simply by continuing to ask "why," beyond the point where it feels reasonable to do so (at least five times). Eventually you will come to the "a-ha" answer that reveals the root cause you're looking for.

I once worked with an intelligent young woman whom we will call Alex. Alex came to me with the primary objective of wanting to know whether or not it was optimal to stick around with her current boyfriend or call it quits. I talked with her about what was and wasn't working in her relationship, and it seemed the relationship was "fine"—not great, not terrible, but not what she truly wanted. She admitted to me that she is a private person who holds her feelings close to her chest, and she didn't want to waste time with someone she knew wasn't "the one."

The trouble was, Alex's typical pattern was to bolt whenever anyone got too close, including friends, boyfriends, or even the person next to her on the subway. She needed distance in order to feel safe.

Using the Why5 method, we continued asking "why" until we got to the root, which turned out to be her relationship with her father. This surprised Alex, as she had not thought about her dad in quite some time, and had undergone plenty of therapy to sort through her feelings about her childhood. But nonetheless, Alex's father is what we found at the root of all of her relationships with men.

Once we discovered the root, we used a powerful forgiveness exercise to release the remaining "unfinished business" with her father, and that's when Alex's heart opened. She broke up with the plain vanilla boyfriend and prepared herself to meet her optimal mate—the one with whom she would be able to share herself at a deeper level than she had ever known possible.

Let's take a look at another example, and this time we'll walk through the process together, so you can see how to apply it to your own pattern.

Alfred is always angry. He's mad at his boss until he loses his job, then he's mad at the economy because he can't find work. He's mad at his wife, though he'd be hard pressed to give you anything substantial as a reason, like she paid the gas bill a day late, or she cooked something he didn't like for dinner. He's mad at the neighbors for being noisy, he's mad at the government for letting gas prices get so high, and he's mad at the television because the one show he likes was just cancelled. Anger is an ongoing theme for Alfred, always present, seething under the surface and eating away at him. He's grouchy and irritable and he snaps at everyone for anything (and nothing).

You know an Alfred, don't you? These people are no fun to be around. But what you might not know is that there are a lot more Alfreds walking around than you may think. Many people harbor anger, but have learned since a very young age that anger is not a "good" thing. Most of us were taught it's not okay to feel mad, so we suppress it. Of course, that doesn't make it go away, but at least no one else can see our Alfred side. We stuff it down and keep it private.

But here's the sticky wicket about emotional stuffing… those buggers always find a way out, and usually in the most unpleasant ways. Your stuffed anger might show up as extra padding around your legs and belly. It might show up as road rage, or impatience with your mother-in-law. Or it might even show up in a sneakier way, like fiery righteousness. Anger disguised as passion sometimes appears to be for a noble cause, like fighting social injustice and the other inequities of our world.

In some ways, the Alfreds of the world are less of a threat than those of us who have deeply suppressed anger. At least we know what we're getting with Alfred. We know he's a cranky old fart, and we expect that of him. But when the mild-mannered accountant and father of three loses his shit and brutally murders the rest of his family, we never see it coming.

Suppressed emotions are scary, and they always find a way to come out. Dear seeker, please consider addressing and resolving your emotions before they surprise you by spilling out at an inopportune time. Let's practice with Why5 now, to get to the underlying root of one of your most persistent emotions.

By the way, you don't have to choose anger for this ride-along. You may still be resistant to hearing that you have suppressed anger, and that's all right for now. For this exercise, choose an emotion that surprises you or catches you off-guard when it arrives, like road rage or crying during a commercial. Pick an emotional pattern you'd like to understand and resolve.

Perhaps you are an easy-going person who flies off the handle when stuck in line, or in traffic. Maybe you are a happy person who gets very sad—bordering on depressed—when you hear about a highly publicized tragedy where many people have died. Maybe religious nuts or GMOs send you off your rocker. Whatever your emotion of choice, take it and map it onto this example of Why5, as we look at Alfred's anger.

NOTE: You will notice that the "five" in Why5 is not a requirement. Generally, when you ask the right questions, it takes between three and eleven "whys" to get to the root. But at some point, the energy of the conversation changes, and you'll know when you strike the root nerve because you will see, hear, or feel a shift.

Alfred (with his usual scowl): "I'm mad as hell."

Yes. Why are you mad as hell?

Alfred (voice rising): "Because this whole country is going to shit."

I see. Why does that make you angry?

Alfred (yelling now): "Because everything is falling apart, and nobody is doing anything about it!"

I can see why that would make anyone angry. But why is it so upsetting to you that nobody is doing anything about it?

Alfred pauses, then after a few moments says in a quiet voice: "Because nobody cares enough to change things."

Ah, okay. Why is it upsetting that nobody cares?

Alfred breaks down. He hasn't cried in twenty-two years and now he's weeping like a baby. "Nobody cares. Nobody cares. Can't they see? Why don't they care?"

Now we have arrived at the root cause. Further discussion reveals that Alfred has suffered some trauma, which might include:

> ➤ The person who loved and cared for him most (perhaps a parent) is gone and ever since they left, he feels as though nobody cares.

- ➤ He did not feel loved as a child. As a coping mechanism, he took on a belief that said, "nobody cares," in order to protect him from the painful realization that nobody cared for him. Now his subconscious mind has spent his life proving to him that it's true.
- ➤ Perhaps something changed in his relationship with his wife: the sex became infrequent or nonexistent, he suspects an affair, etc. Or it could be as small and seemingly insignificant as she stopped doing something nice for him, like cooking his favorite foods, buying him gifts, or kissing him good-night. This trigger is bringing his anger that "nobody cares" to a head.

Looking at Alfred, you might never have guessed that his anger was caused by a belief that "nobody cares." The angrier he grew over the years, the more the people in his life pulled away from him, reinforcing his underlying belief that nobody cares. Until this belief is shifted, Alfred will withdraw deeper and deeper, in an attempt to insulate himself against the cold, cruel, uncaring world.

Alternatively, Alfred could work with a gifted healer to release his deeply ingrained belief that nobody cares. This would free him to enjoy a life of deeply caring and intimate relationships. When these changes occur, they are profound. Can you see how this clearing stuff is truly life changing?

NOTE: The Why5 exercise does not always produce tears. I have seen the shift—the one where you know you've gotten to the *real* why underneath it all—reveal itself as surprise, an epiphany, goose bumps, and even laughter. For sure, you will notice a shift in the mood or emotion or demeanor of the person answering the "why" questions as soon as you uncover that root "why."

Take the time now to work through one of your emotional patterns and use Why5 to discover the root cause. After you do this a few times with a few different scenarios, you'll quickly get the hang of it and the Why5 will become a powerful tool in your clearing arsenal.

Method #3: Paper Chase

This method requires pen, paper, a timer (like the one on your smartphone, the microwave, or the old-fashioned wind-up kind), and a quiet place to yourself. Begin with a fresh sheet of paper and at the top write:

This is the answer I have been looking for.

Then set the timer for fifteen minutes and start writing. Do not stop for any reason until that timer goes off. Even if you wind up writing "this is dumb," and "I don't know," or "my hand hurts," it's okay, just keep writing. While the timer is ticking, the pen is "hot" and you take all of this time to write swiftly and without judgment. Remember Dory in the Pixar film *Finding Nemo*? Well, instead of "just keep swimming," Dory is singing to "just keep writing." If at any point you get stuck or hit a nerve and you are tempted to stop and ponder what you just uncovered, remember Dory and "just keep writing." You can use this prompt to keep you going:

I am writing this so that I can...

Here's an example. Margaret was looking for answers as to why she couldn't get her husband on the same page. The kids were out of control, the house was a mess, the finances were not in order, and Margaret was tired of always having to be the responsible parent. She had grown frustrated and was ready to make some changes, but her husband was too entrenched in "the way thing had always been." This is an example of what Margaret created with her paper chase:

This is the answer I have been looking for.
I don't know what Bill's problem is. Really, it seems so obvious to me that we've lost all sense of order and discipline in this house, but how can I get any changes to stick if he refuses to change? He is just being stubborn about everything. Maybe he doesn't trust me. Maybe he buys into that old way of thinking that says the man is always right and the wife is just a pretty face. No, I don't think that's it, and I don't know what it is, but he is really pissing me off.

I have tried to talk to him about this so many times, and he acts like he's listening, but then he just goes right back to his same old bad habits. What am I doing wrong here?

Just then, Margaret got stuck. After a short pause, she imagined little blue Dory singing, "just keep writing," so she wrote:

I am writing this so that I can *find an answer to get through to Bill so that we can be happy together. Wait, is that what I really want? Maybe it's time I left Bill. How would that work if I started over? I know the kids would miss him, because he's such a great dad, but I can't stay here any more. Is it selfish of me to want my own life, a different life? I don't know what to do.*

Margaret noticed her mind drifting again, so she used the prompt again:

I am writing this so that I can *figure out what I really want. Huh. Now that I think about it, I've never in my life gotten what I wanted. I didn't want kids, and yet here I am with four. Sure, I love them more than anything, but it wasn't my choice to be a mother. I definitely didn't want to be stuck in this small town with these same people all the time. I used to have dreams. I wanted to be somebody. I wonder if it's too late. I wonder if I still can.*

Now Margaret was getting into a rhythm. She would write and uncover a hidden truth, then when she felt herself wanting to stop and chew on the new discovery, she'd repeat the prompt and it would spark a new thought that kept her going. The timer continued to count down while Dory reminded her to "just keep writing."

By the time Margaret's timer went off, she had her answer plus a whole page of things to ponder about herself, her marriage, and her life. She decided she would give her husband an ultimatum, and this time, it wasn't a bluff or a feeble attempt at gaining his attention. Margaret began planning out her options in case Bill didn't get on board, which would mean good-bye.

In my experience, I have learned that it is very difficult for a spouse to say "no" to you when you have made up your mind and you have taken the time to plan for contingencies and alternatives. There's a huge difference between planting your feet firmly and taking a stand vs. crying wolf in a tentative, testing-the-waters way, and most partners can sniff out the difference in an instant. If they can't, you're better off without them anyway. But if you deliver an ultimatum, be prepared to carry out the consequences if the other person says "fine by me."

This hot-pen paper chase will help you discover hidden truths inside of you, and when that timer finally goes off, you may even find you want to keep writing for a while more. Either way, when you're finished, you'll have a heap of insights to chew on, and you'll be all the wiser for taking this time to delve into your hidden truths.

If you want answers, use the paper chase hot-pen technique with the recommended prompts and you'll have your answers within just fifteen minutes.

A Word About Past Lives

According to well-known Law of Attraction teacher Abraham-Hicks, past lives don't matter. Abraham advises us to focus only on the *now* in the present lifetime.

That's all fine and good, unless old stuff from your past lives is affecting your ability to be happy and to manifest freely today. No matter how crappy your spouse treats you, you can't leave the relationship if you have a pact or a sacred contract in place from a prior lifetime; at least not until you dissolve that agreement. This is just one example of the many ways that our past lives can create unpleasant patterns in this lifetime. I wish it were true that we could only focus on this lifetime and create all that we desire, but I've seen far too much evidence to the contrary.

Don't get me wrong; I understand the rationale behind Abraham-Hicks' dismissive remarks about past lives. It's not helpful to dwell in the past, or to believe there are karmic debts to be fulfilled, or to sigh with the burden of thinking you must clear your experiences from a thousand prior lifetimes.

But just because we cannot remember all of our past lives, this doesn't mean that they aren't still affecting us today. Some of the crap that's rocking your world right now is garbage you've dragged behind you for hundreds of lifetimes. We're talking *really* old stuff.

Consider this: if past lives truly have no effect on the present lifetime, how do you explain:

- babies with birth defects born to healthy, conscientious energetically "aware" parents
- stillbirths
- conjoined twins
- SIDS (sudden infant death syndrome)
- Down's syndrome
- anything on the Autism spectrum
- fears and phobias with no originating source within this lifetime
- addictions and food sensitivities
- ADHD and ADD
- mental imbalances that begin at birth or extremely young ages, such as bipolar disorder, manic depression, multiple personalities, etc.

The truth is nearly all of us (except for a smattering of "new souls") have all been there, done that, and then designed, bought, sold, stole, shredded, tie-dyed, and burned the t-shirts. We have done it all, baby. I'm sorry to tell you that you have been the murderer, the victim, the accomplice, the fake alibi, the real alibi, the judge, the attorney, the jury, and the prison guard. You've probably even been the cockroach that lived in the prison. No wonder you are such a wise soul; you have seriously been around the block!

And every trauma, every betrayal, every unresolved heartache is living and lurking in your energy field today and affecting your day-to-day well-being. If you don't believe me, use your Truth Testing method to check in and ask: All things considered, is it true that my past lives are affecting my present life? I promise not to say "I told you so." Well, not out loud anyway.

Now do you see why I'm so passionate about this clearing stuff? This is important shizzle!

Chap-Recap #3

Food for Thought:

1. The core issue stems from the originating incident. This the moment you made a decision or choice, adopted a belief, or created an agreement that is still with you today.
2. It is *essential* to go back to the originating incident and resolve it, otherwise the blocks will resurface.
3. We all have destructive patterns. When you're the one repeating the pattern, it can be hard to spot, at least until you become ready to shift it.
4. Being *ready* to release the block is essential. Until you are ready and willing, it will not shift.
5. When you've identified the pattern, the next step is to ask: what emotion, thought, fear, or limiting belief is always present when the pattern occurs?
6. You can use the Why5 method to continue asking "why" until you get to the underlying root.
7. The Paper Chase hot-pen technique is a useful tool to tap into your subconscious and discover hidden truths.
8. Some of the crap that's rocking your world right now is garbage you've dragged behind you for hundreds of lifetimes. How many more lifetimes would you like to carry it with you? Now is a great time to release it for good.
9. You are a wise soul because you have lived many lifetimes and experienced life from countless perspectives.

Action Plan:

1. For the next few days, practice noticing patterns in your life. Do you tend to eat the same foods? Hang out with the same group of people? What expression do you use far too much? Where are you stuck in a rut? Which emotions tend to trip you up and surprise you when they come up out of the blue? Make notes about your observations.

2. Practice Praxis: Choose one of the patterns you identified in action item #1 above and then try your hand at Why5 to practice getting to the root cause of the pattern.
3. If you struggle with Why5, use the Paper Chase method to find the root cause. Be sure to write it down, because we'll work on clearing it in ChapRecap #4. Remember to use the prompts if you get stuck.
4. What are your thoughts and feelings about the "Past Lives" explanation? Use your notebook to write about whatever comes up for you around this topic.
5. Notice if you have any resistance to anything you've read so far. Take a few minutes to jot down your thoughts in your notebook.

Amy Scott Grant

CHAPTER FOUR

Step 2. Clear the Underlying Block

When you get clear, you get results.

~Amy Scott Grant

The next step in this three-step process is to actually clear the underlying block. You might be surprised to learn that there are as many methods for clearing as there are people who are interested in clearing. Well, maybe not quite that many, but there are a crapload for sure, along with the ongoing development and discovery of new methods, as well as enhancements of old methods.

Beware any healer who tells you they have found "the one tried and true method." My vast experience has proven this:

There is no one true way.

Likewise, there is no *one and only* soul mate for you, no one perfect career for you, no one perfect version of your body, no one ideal hairstyle and truly, no missed opportunities. It is actually impossible for you to "miss out" on anything, you amazingly infinite being. As the profoundly succinct Florence Scovel Shinn wrote back in 1925, *there is no loss in Divine Mind.*

There are many paths to healing, many paths to clarity, and many paths to freedom. Since this is a 1-2-3 guide, I will explain

49

and invite you to experiment with just three of these myriad methods, and if you like them enough to want to try some more, reach out to me. I teach all the methods I've sourced, and I'm sourcing and testing new ones all the time. I would love nothing more than to share my discoveries with you. This is exactly why I created my HIY Heal It Yourself series, where you can learn tons of healing methods and you can also learn to source and invent your own.

What's the opposite of a one-trick pony? I don't know, but whatever it is, this is what becomes available to you once you open yourself to learning how to clear blocks, doubts, fears, and limiting beliefs. In my courses, I teach many, many methods, and I do so because I know they won't all resonate with you. Likely, you will prefer just one of the three I'll teach you in this book, and that's fine. As my dad always says, "it takes all kinds," and I like to think he wasn't just talking about people. We all love options, so why should healing be any different?

I'm not the kind of healer who thinks my way is the right way or the only way, or that you have to do it just the way I show you. Poppycock to all that! My ego is totally chill if your work winds up surpassing my own, and I would love nothing more than for my students, clients, readers, and fans to invent even better, more efficient methods than mine. When that happens, everyone wins. Plus, it would prove to me that you took the teaching to heart, that you tapped yourself into Source, and you listened to the guidance you got. And if you felt inspired to share your findings with me, then you have truly made my day because I will have been enriched by your presence as the student becomes the teacher.

One of my favorite sayings is "Be still and know that I am God." I grew up in a very Catholic family, but all throughout my childhood I loved that comforting and soothing thought. Several years ago, I heard that statement for the first time in ages and it rocked my world because this time, I heard it in an entirely different way.

I was sitting in a Unity church in Tennessee where there is a huge stained glass window that says "Be still" and I almost burst out laughing as I realized, "oh my gawd. Be still, and *I am God!*"

What if "Be still and know that I am God" *isn't* about God saying: "Hey you there. Yes you, lowly human. Be still and know that I am God. That's right, I'm the powerful one. I'm in charge." And that is supposed to relax you and bring you comfort.

But what if—just what if—it's really telling you: "Relax and be still. Know that *you* are God, and is there anything that God can't handle? Nope. Which means there is nothing that YOU can't handle. So chill out, babe. Have another lemonade and kick your feet up, you *got* this."

It's amazing what a change in perspective can do. Talk about your moment of clarity, right? Yes, Virginia there is a God. And she is YOU. By the way, you are also Santa Claus, the Prosperity Fairy, and the Soul Mate en Route to Someone Wonderful.

You could be feeling a lot of different emotions as you read this. Old religious dogma from your childhood may be speaking up, calling this blasphemy or something equally as unforgivable. You might be experiencing doubt. Me? God? How can that be? Or perhaps what you are reading is resonating to the deepest levels of your being and you feel your skin bubble up in "truth bumps" with a hint of the unmistakable nausea of Truth in the pit of your stomach. You might be anywhere in-between. Whatever you are feeling, just try to observe it, without judgment.

Need a thought-break? Take a few minutes to chew through some of the thoughts and feelings rattling around your head and heart. When you're ready to try on the possibility that you are God, then pick up this book again and continue as we dive into a trio of powerful clearing methods. Enjoy the pause, but don't wait too long, because I know you have some crap to clear and you'd like to get that handled sooner rather than later.

* * *

Welcome back.

Ready to jump into some clearing? Wonderful! First, let me tell you that if you already consider yourself to be an intuitive person, this may seem almost *too* easy to you (because it is). Very intuitive people often ask me, "Really? Is that all there is to it?" My elegant response: "Yup."

The trick is staying connected and plugged into your intuition instead of getting tripped up in analysis paralysis. Hint: analysis occurs in your head-zone, whereas intuition does not. I had a client once who was always stuck in her head. When she attended one of my retreats, I was amazed to observe her in person because she literally could not answer a question without touching her head in some way. So if you consider yourself the analytical type, you might want to keep an eye out for that pattern, too.

If you already consider yourself to be intuitive, the clearing part is super-simple because you just check in and ask, "Is it optimal to clear this?" If you get yes, then ask, "How does this want to be cleared?" and then complete whatever actions you are guided to take. Yup, it is really that simple. That is the very same process by which I sourced a significant number of my clearing methods.

It's also how I keep inventing new clearing methods. I continue to work on myself, day-by-day, month-by-month, and year-by-year. I believe I am a work in progress and I am committed to squeezing every drop of awesomeness out of this lifetime. I love results, I love productivity, and I love efficiency. The way I look at it, the more crap I clear in this lifetime, the more awesomesauce my next lifetime will have.

I'm not saying you have to think that way. Go with whatever inspires you. Maybe you are inspired to create a better life, or more money, or an amazing relationship, or something better for your children or your family. Maybe you love games, and clearing as many blocks as you can is the ultimate game to play. Or maybe you just want to get rid of the damn migraines, or anxiety attacks, or the need to consume three glasses of wine every night. You know, "just to wine—er, *wind* down from the day." Whatever the reason, let yours inspire and motivate you to keep going when you come up against a tough block that doesn't seem to want to budge (we'll cover that later).

By continuing to work on myself (identifying blocks, asking how best to clear them, then clearing them), I frequently discover new ways of clearing. I know I'm onto something good when a similar issue arises for one or more of my private clients or students, giving me the opportunity to test the new technique on someone other than myself. I share the new clearing style with them, they get results, and soon the new method weaves its way into my teachings. It's like the circle of life for clearing work. Otherwise known as "progress."

I'm grinning even now as I write this, not only because my cornball sense of humor still cracks me up, but because until I discovered this healing work, I had always been the person who grew bored and restless within two years of any career move. But healing work is ever-evolving, ever-expanding and after more than a decade of this, I am amazed at how far my work has come and still, there's never a dull moment. This is the first time in my life I can honestly say I can't imagine ever growing bored. There's just too much left to explore, too much more to discover, and the people I work with inspire me in a way I have never before experienced. That may or may not be the case with you, but if you are inspired to grow, to become more than you've ever dreamed possible, and if this work has touched or moved you in any way, then I am happy. I know the ripple magic effect that this work can create as your shift ripples out into your immediate circle, and eventually, throughout the world.

Did you know that changing the world is what you were signing up for when you picked out this book? No pressure, of course.

The thought of changing the world is inspiring to some but intimidating to others. Don't worry about the world just yet. For the time being, just focus on healing yourself. Because I know you may find this hard to believe, but in healing yourself you are beginning to change the world. If you think that sounds impossible or esoteric and lofty, ask me about Ripple Magic and prepare to have your mind blown. In the meantime, let's get back to clearing.

We covered the clearing process for those who already have some sense of their own intuitive powers, but what if you do not consider yourself an intuitive person? Don't sweat it, doll! I'm going to walk you through three easy methods step-by-step.

Method #1: Cord Cutting

Cord cutting is not new, nor did I invent it (well, at least not in *this* lifetime). It's difficult to find information about the origin of cord cutting, most likely because there are so many variations of the process and it's been around for so very long. It's likely that the practice is based on the clipping of the umbilical cord between mother and child. If that's the case, the human race has missed the boat because nearly everyone who comes to me for healing work has mommy issues, whether they know it or not.

When I first learned about cord cutting, I was disappointed in its ephemeral nature. I can remember it like it was yesterday. I had received a particularly disturbing email from a friend who needed a check up from the neck up and was subsequently pushing away all of her long-time friends, including me. Her email to me was harsh to say the least—accusatory, inflammatory, and vastly untrue. Worst of all, she refused to get on the phone with me, and some issues just can't be sorted out effectively through electronic means, which left me with no way to work things out with her. This was the end of a long-term friendship and I was a tangle of emotions. There was no way to get closure since she refused to talk to me. I felt incomplete and deeply wounded.

I called another healer for guidance, and she walked me through the cord-cutting process. Instantly, I felt better, at least at first. About twenty minutes later, I found myself back in the soup. Emotions flared up again as I remembered the hurtful things that were said in the email. But I had done the cord cutting, so why did it come back? This made no sense to me.

I called up the healer who had performed the cord cutting. The conversation went something like this:

Me: "Hey, it's Amy. Something's wrong, I don't think that cord cutting worked."

Other Healer: "Really? Why do you say that?"

Me: "Because I'm pissed off again and it's all back in my head."

Other Healer: "Oh honey, you might have to repeat that cord cutting two thousand times before you don't think about her anymore."

Me, speechless, for the first time ever. Awkward silence.

Other Healer: "I once had someone who had to keep doing cord cutting for several days before she was completely over the incident."

Me: "Yeah, that's not gonna work for me. Gotta go."

Just so you know, repeating the same clearing over a period of several days is *not* effective energy work. That's simply a by-product of "time heals all wounds."

I then made it my mission to create a way to make cord cuttings permanent, which I did. It was a very temporary mission, but I accomplished it, nonetheless. Seriously, who has time to repeat a clearing two thousand times? Maybe it's just me, but I have an extremely low tolerance for repetition. I am forever looking for ways to streamline the process. I barely even travel to the same place more than once because I'm always thinking about how many *other* amazing places are out there that I haven't yet seen or experienced.

I figure if I'm lucky, I've got another forty to fifty years ahead of me. The more efficient I can be right now, especially with regards to improving my life and the life of my family, then the more of life I can experience with whatever time I've got left.

Which means there's no way in hell I'm going to be repeating the same clearing exercise two thousand (or even two dozen) times for the same damn issue! We are burnin' daylight so let's get these clearings handled, once-and-done.

Permanent cord cutting in three easy steps:

Step 1: Visualize the setup
Step 2: Cut the cord
Step 3: Let it go

Simple, right? Let me flesh out the full details for you, in classic Spiritual Ass Kicker style, so that you can make it permanent and only have to do each cord cutting once.

NOTE: In very rare cases (perhaps seven times out of a hundred) the cord cutting has to be repeated a second time. But the other 93% of the time, it is permanent and you are freed forever. Nice, right? You're damn right it is. It's downright amazeballs.

Before we begin, it is essential that you know with whom you are cutting cords. If you've identified the pattern, it should be obvious whom you are cutting the cord with. In case it's not, let's revisit some of our prior examples.

Remember me, before my image makeover? My cord cutting would have been with comfortable, frumpy me—the "mommyhood" version of me that I had outwardly become.

Remember suppressed, suicidal me, afraid to be my true Spiritual Ass Kicker self because I was taught early on that it was unacceptable? That cord cutting would have been with the version of myself that was afraid to just be me.

I did cut the cord with Calamity Jane (the batshit crazy client who I never should have taken on). If it ain't congruent, don't do it.

How about Becky the apologizer? She could have cut the cord with the word "sorry," or with the root cause for her need to apologize, or with the "sorry" version of herself that insists on apologizing for who she is.

Alex, who was on the fence about her meh boyfriend could have cut the cord with her father, who was the root of all her issues with individuals of the male persuasion.

Speaking of daddy issues, Luke could have cut the cord with Lord Vader. But that would not have produced as satisfying an ending as what we actually saw.

The ever-angry Alfred could cut the cord with the catalyst that prompted him to adopt the belief that "nobody cares." Alternatively, he could cut the cord with nameless, faceless Nobody who doesn't care. Once Alfred is freed from that, he is free to care or not care, without having to be perpetually pissed off that others don't seem to care enough.

Disenchanted Margaret could cut the cord with hubby Bill and then be able to see clearly as to whether or not to stay with him or leave him and move on. In fact, I would strongly recommend that she execute a cord cutting before she delivers that ultimatum, as it will allow her to be more neutral about his decision.

You could even cut the cord with your ego, how 'bout that?

As you can see, cord cutting doesn't always have to be with a person. It could be with the amazing job you didn't get, the house you didn't qualify for, the money you lost in that bad investment, the one who got away, or even the book you've decided not to write after all. Can we have a moment of silence for that book which will never be? Thank you.

But why would you want to cut the cord with someone you still want in your life?

Because cord cutting doesn't mean they go away forever.

Sure, sometimes it does, but not all the time. With my permanent cord cutting method, there are some basic guidelines for maximum efficacy:

First do no harm. Like the Hippocratic oath, we seek the best for all parties involved when we cut cords. Cord cutting will not be effective if you want the person to get the hell away from you, or burn in hell, or other choice words I'll omit in order to keep this book relatively PG-13. When you can feel completely *neutral* about the person or situation; when you want only the best for the other person; when you simply wish to be free from the cords that have bound you and no longer serve either of you; this is when cord cutting works and works amazingly well.

It's about release, not revenge.

When we cut cords, we release all that no longer serves, with the highest and best intention for all involved.

Never cut cords from a place of spite or anger. If you cannot cut the cords with love, then you must at the very least be neutral about it; otherwise, you will find yourself right back where you started, as though the cord cutting never happened. Remember the weeds that got cut at ground level? They're back in no time, unlike the weeds that were completely removed, down to the roots.

How can you get to a space of love or neutrality, after what this person did to you? Do your forgiveness work. If you don't already have a preferred method for forgiveness work, use my Ripple Magic Forgiveness Clearing. Sorry "Shark Tank" sharks, it's not sales that cures all, it's *forgiveness*.

Cut only the cords that no longer serve. I have cut cords with my children—yes, my beloved children whom I love and adore and admire and cherish! But this ain't our first rodeo together. We have all dragged some crap into this lifetime from our past lives together. This became evident to me in the form of repetitive arguments, irrational fears and worries, and unfounded frustrations. Upon deeper perspective and in the interest of household harmony, I found it was time to let go of the past betrayals and unmet expectations, so that we could be free to love each other without all that ancient crap muddying the waters.

I have cut cords with my husband over a number of various issues. He and I have had many lifetimes together, but in every single instance except this lifetime, we were on opposite sides of the fence. Can you believe that? This is the first lifetime where he and I have chosen to play on the same team. Imagine how many hatchets we've buried in our nearly twenty years together, many of which didn't even originate in this lifetime! The whole marriage/past lives thing is just fascinating to me. When we consider how many couples are in therapy yet can't make any real progress in their relationship, we can see it's because they're only dealing with issues from their childhood and their relationship *in this lifetime*. Epic fail.

When we cut a cord, we cut all that no longer serves, with the intention that all the love, the fond memories, and everything positive remains.

How will you know what no longer serves? You don't have to know. Isn't that wonderful? You can simply hold the intention that all that no longer serves is permanently released as part of the cord cutting. Intend it and so it is. It's one of the inherent beauties of clearing work. Now let's take an in-depth look at the 1-2-3 of the cord cutting process.

Step 1: Visualize the setup

Begin by imagining you are standing face to face with the person or thing you wish to release. Usually about two to four feet apart is sufficient. Next, visualize the cords that connect the two of you. Notice the cords and where they are attached. It is not necessary to interpret or analyze this, but simply to notice. For example, if you were cutting cords with your mother (which I highly recommend…like it or not, we all have our mommy issues. Believe me, a whole world of freedom opens up once you clear these) then you might see thick, rope-like cords running between her heart and yours. Or you might see light, ethereal strings in a braid from her heart to your belly. In some cases, there are multiple cords running to and from different locations. There is no right answer here, so whatever you see is perfect. You don't need to write it down or judge what you see, but simply notice what pops into your awareness as you stand before the person or thing.

Next, is there anything you'd like to say before you cut the cord? Often there's nothing to say, while other times it's something like "I forgive you" or "I release you and ask that you release me" or "thank you and good-bye" or "I wish you well." If there's something you want to say, say it now. This helps to create a permanent release with complete closure.

The last step in the setup is to choose a tool, any tool you want. Keep in mind that we want to cut the cords in one fell swoop, so don't pick a hacksaw, a nail file, or anything that is going to require multiple strokes to sever. I've seen clients use tools like a giant scissors (the kind you would see at a grand opening ribbon cutting), an axe, a blow torch, a laser, a machete, a very sharp knife, a light saber (excellent choice, young Jedi), a chainsaw, a hatchet, a fairy godmother's magic wand and all sorts of other tools. Notice I call this a "tool" and not a weapon, in keeping with the idea that you are releasing from a space of love or at least neutrality, as opposed to a space of anger, fear or hatred. Choose any tool you wish as long as you can get all the cords in one swift motion. Once you can imagine your tool, you are ready to move onto step two.

Step 2: Cut the cord

When I walk someone through this exercise, I first ask if they are ready. When they say yes, I ask them to take a deep breath, then I count down slowly: three, two, one, *cut*. I don't know how essential the countdown is, but it does add a certain panache to the experience.

The key to remember is when you cut, make one clean and swift cut. You don't want to be sawing or hacking away like you're a lumberjack. This is to be done in one fell swoop, and if you've got cords running every which way between you and what/whomever we're cutting cords with, then gather them all up into your hand before you raise your tool, so that you can get everything in one slice or snip or whack, depending on your tool of choice.

This next part is essential in making a cord-cutting permanent. When you cut, imagine that the cords (especially the part that runs between your body and the point where you cut) either disappear entirely, or fall to the ground and then disappear. I've had clients tell me the cords fell to the ground then turned to snakes and slithered out of sight, while other clients have imagined the cords turning into pixie dust the instant the cut is made. Others had to wave a magic wand to get the cut cords to disappear, or infuse them with glowing light, but the important thing is that once cut, the cords fall away, are no longer connected to you, and disappear forever. That is key.

Step 3: Let it go

The last step is symbolic of total and permanent release, and if you see something fishy here, then it's a good indication that you weren't completely neutral when you cut the cord. Once you cut the cords and see them fall away and disappear, watch the person (or thing) across from you float up and away from you, like a helium balloon set free. Watch until he/she/it shrinks away to just a speck, then disappears entirely. Incidentally, most people see the person or thing rise up and to the left, but that's not a hard-and-fast rule. When it's completely gone, you are done.

If you see something different happening, there may be more to do to complete this cord cutting, or it could be that you weren't entirely ready to release. One example of this would be if you cut the cords and they disappear, but the person won't go away, or they appear angry or hurt. Or they rise up into the air, but they're still tethered to you somehow. If this happens, do some more forgiveness work and then repeat the cord cutting later.

Occasionally, something unusual may happen when you cut the cord. For example, when cutting the cord with someone who will still remain in your life, I have often seen the other person multiply into "twins" when the cord is cut. One twin rises up and away, while the other twin crosses over to stand side by side with the person doing the cutting. A hug or arm around the shoulder sometimes follows. The main thing to notice is how you feel at the end of the cord cutting. At the very least, you should feel neutral, and at the very best, you would experience a sense of peace or freedom. Some people sigh when the cord cutting is complete.

How can you tell if it's really, really, really finished?

Notice how you feel over the next few days. In many cases, the cord cutting is so thorough that you may forget you ever had an issue with this person or thing or circumstance. May sound crazy, but it's happened to me more than once. Incidentally, that's true of any kind of clearing, not just cord cuttings.

Therefore, I recommend putting a tickler on your calendar for a few days out, which might say, "check in to see how I feel about _____." This will remind you in case the cord cutting was so effective that you've forgotten the issue ever existed. If it's incomplete, you will still have adverse feelings about the person or situation, or more likely, it will show up in your space before you even get to that tickler reminder.

Of note, I have spent several pages explaining the cord cutting process. I prefer to be thorough, rather than leave you with a bunch of unanswered questions. In reality, the entire cord cutting process may take as little as a couple of minutes. But now that you understand the full process, and you know how to make it permanent, you are empowered to do your own permanent cord cutting. So if my in-depth explanations are not to your liking, you'd better learn to skim if you're going to survive the rest of this book. But if you're like most of the folks who are attracted to my work and my writing, you're appreciative of the extra details, because now you know exactly what to do and how to do it. Voilá.

Method #2: Pack Your Bags, We're Taking a (Mental) Trip

The second method I'm going to show you is somewhat difficult to explain in written form. But, in classic Spiritual Ass Kicker style, I will do my best to be detailed and thorough, and provide you with an alternative option. You can find an audio version of this guided visualization here on my website. https://s3.amazonaws.com/GetClearBook/ReleasingAnger.mp3

That is not a published link, and is intended only for those who have purchased this book *and* read all the way up to this point. Consider it a little reward for your diligence and commitment (remember lagniappe?). You're welcome.

Guided visualization is exactly what it sounds like, and the good news is that you don't need a guru or healing expert to walk you through it. You can actually create your own guided visualizations by simply opening your connection to Source and seeing what comes through. I can almost hear all the highly intuitive types saying, "well, duh" and if that's you, then good for you. You can skip this section and listen to the audio if you like. But if that feels out of your reach at the moment, keep reading and prepare to be edu-muh-cated.

Now before you tell me you can't visualize, consider that the cord cutting exercise we just did is a guided visualization. Likewise, every time you replay a conversation or scenario in your head (I can't believe she said that; I can't believe I did that; this is what I should have said/done instead; oh no, what if such-and-such happens?), that's a visualization. It's far easier than you think, and if you have a block around visualization, clear it. It's a powerful tool that can serve you in countless ways. Plus you might be stuck in your headspace again, so check on that.

A guided visualization for the purposes of clearing is a simple and effective way to release your blocks. Think of it as lucid dreaming. You create an imaginary scenario, an imaginary world (or one that's oddly familiar) and you walk yourself through a pleasant process that concludes with the release of your block, doubt, fear, or limiting belief.

Remember Alex the Indecisive? We used a guided visualization (which later became the Ripple Magic Forgiveness Clearing) to release her remaining blocks around her father. For the purpose of this example, let's use Angry Alfred and create a visualization around releasing anger.

I'm going to talk (write) you through this visualization. Yup, I totally appreciate the irony that I will first ask you to close your eyes. (But how can I read if my eyes are closed? It's a koan, like "what is the sound of one hand clapping?") I believe you will find value in first reading through this process, and then listening to the audio, or creating your own visualization.

* * *

"Releasing Anger"
Transcription of Audio Clearing

Begin by taking a couple of deep breaths and getting settled and relaxed, right where you are. It's fine if you are sitting or lying down. I'm going to walk you through a very simple guided visualization exercise.

As you breathe and get comfortable, allow whatever you are sitting or lying on to fully support you. Just sink down into it. That's good.

Now I invite you to remember a time when you were really angry. It could be something that happened recently, or maybe it's something from your childhood or adolescence.

It could be a big event, like finding out your spouse cheated on you, or it could be a small event, like being treated poorly in a restaurant or a store.

The magnitude of the event itself is not what's important here; what's important is to recall a time when your anger was intense.

Maybe you thought for a moment you wanted to strangle somebody or punch your fist through a wall. That would be a good example of what we're looking for here.

Have you got that time? I promise this will be the only unpleasant part; remembering this time when you were so angry.

As you recall that memory, notice what's lighting up inside your body. There will be one prominent spot in your body where this anger seems to flare. It could be in the front of your head. It could be in your throat – maybe you feel your throat closing now as it did then.

It could be in your chest, maybe you feel a tightness in your chest. It could be in the pit of your stomach. It could be someplace else entirely, but notice the precise location where that anger appears to flare.

Turn your attention to the anger, to the location of it. The circumstances will start to fall away, but pay attention to the anger itself, and see if you can notice without judgment or analysis. For example, what characteristics does it have? Is it a certain color? Is it dense and dark and gray? Or is it fiery red, or is it white hot? I'm just giving you examples; there's no right answer here, and you don't have to recall any of this when we're done. Just be present with me in the moment, right now.

What color is your anger? How intense is that color? Does the color appear static, or does it change, perhaps pulsating? How big is the anger? How dense? Is it a tight, nubby little ball, packed solid? Or is it a bigger tangle of wires? What's the weight and the density of it? Are there any other physical descriptions you can give of this anger? For example, does it feel hot to the touch? Does it move or breathe? Notice all that you can about this anger.

When you're ready, use your hand (the energetic version of your hand) to reach into your body and pull out the anger. Pull the whole piece of it out until it's hovering right in front of you. Notice it. Be curious. Explore it with your eyes, in your mind.

This is what rocked your world that day. This is what threw you off your game. This is what changed you in that moment. Maybe you have some thoughts about it. Maybe you find it funny, or strange, or curious, or maddening, that this – what you see in front of you – is what flared up when that thing happened.

Now you have a choice. On the one hand, you could keep the thing. You could reach out with your hand and stick it back in your body, and continue to carry it with you.

Or, on the other hand, you could release it. You could let it go so that it will never be a part of you in this way again.

Make your decision now.

If you've decided to keep it, go ahead and place it back in your body and then just relax until the end of this visualization.

But if you've chosen to let it go, listen carefully because I will give you instructions.

Right now, you should not be touching the object. It should be hovering just in front of you, and your hands are free. Here's what we are going to do: I'm going to count you down, "3-2-1 go," and when I say "go," you're going to put your hands around the object without touching it and you're going to encompass it in a big bubble, a bubble that is unbreakable by you. Then, when I say "push," you will push that bubble out and away from you. Then it will return to Source where it will be transformed into beautiful, perfect Light.

And if it is ever to return to you, it can only return to you in its perfect form (beautiful, perfect Light) that can only come to you as blessings and love.

Here we go, are you ready?

Three, two, one, go.

Without touching, shape your arms and your hands around the object and completely cover it in a bubble. Enclose it fully. When I say "push," you will push it out and away from you.

Three, two, one, push.

See it go? Way, way, way out, until it disappears! Tiny as a pinprick and then boom, it's gone.

Feel the freedom, the lightness, the weight that has been lifted. No longer are you carrying this particular burden of anger. And you can come back and repeat this exercise as other forms of anger are identified, and as you remember other betrayals and injustices from your past.

The more anger you release, the lighter and freer you will feel. The more liberated you will be. Take a very deep breath and when you do, this time breathe in a sense of freedom and liberation, and then let it out slowly. As you let out this deep breath, you release tension from your body, tension you didn't even realize you were carrying all this time. Notice how you feel right now. Happy, free, peaceful, neutral?

You've done it! You've released this anger!

Know that when you are ready, you can return your awareness to your surroundings. You can stretch and open your eyes, but you don't have to. You can stay in this relaxed and peaceful space as long as you wish.

You could even fall asleep right now if you wanted to…but perhaps you should stay awake long enough to finish the rest of this chapter.

* * *

How was it? Did you enjoy the experience? Did you discover anything new about yourself? Take a few minutes now to process what you've just discovered, and to explore how you now feel about anger, or the specific relationship or situation you worked on. Take a journal break before you continue with the next method.

Method #3: The Trusty Pendy

This third method is very simple and stress-free but it requires one tool: a pendulum. If you don't currently own a pendulum, you can order a very cool one at www.custompendulums.com or you can fashion one from objects around your house. If you're new to using a pendulum, the easiest thing to use as a substitute is a pendant or a ring on a necklace or chain. I personally use whatever happens to be handy, but for the purposes of healing, you want something with enough weight on the swinging part to be clear and visible when it moves vs. when it stands still.

In the next chapter, we'll look at more ways to use a pendulum but for now, we're just going to keep things simple as I show you how to use a pendulum for clearing.

There are many ways to use spiritual tools for clearing blocks. This is one of my favorite ways to teach people to clear, because it requires no intuitive understanding on your part. This means anyone, at any stage of their journey, with any degree of intuition (including none) can successfully do this.

Once you have identified the specific block you'd like to clear, hold it in your mind as you touch your throat lightly with your dominant hand and say aloud, "I am willing to release this. I am willing to release this. I am willing to release this." Then pick up your pendulum and hold it so that it can swing freely, while you close your eyes and relax. Do your best to clear your mind and as thoughts arise, gently let them go and return to a silent mental space. As you hold the pendulum, it may swing wildly, or gently, and it may even change directions or move in an elliptical fashion. Whatever it does is fine, just relax and let it do the work for you. Eventually, the pendulum will stop swinging and become completely still. At this point, you may get confirmation that the clearing is complete, which could appear as:

- the spontaneous desire to open your eyes and move, at which point you notice the pendulum has stopped moving
- a yawn, sneeze, shiver, sigh, goose bumps, or other physical reaction
- the pendulum becomes very still, then shakes or vibrates
- a certainty or inner knowing that the clearing is now complete
- a fleeting thought or wondering whether the clearing is complete, immediately followed by a sound (the phone or doorbell rings, or the ever-silent dog suddenly barks, or perhaps you hear the "ping" of an incoming text message)

Some people find they receive the same message in the same way, to indicate a complete clearing. For example, my pendulum stops then shakes when the clearing is done. When I am not using a tool for clearing, I spontaneously yawn when the clearing is complete.

How long does it take to clear?

Some clearings move very quickly (a minute or two) while others take significantly longer (upwards of twenty minutes). You will usually find that the more clearings you do, the faster they become. At this point, many of my clearings are nearly instantaneous. But remember, I have been at this for over a decade, so do not grow discouraged if your clearings take a very long time at first. Even if it takes a half hour to do one clearing, that's better than continuing to live with the pain of the block, isn't it?

Now you are armed with three powerful healing tools. Before you go hog wild and attack every block, doubt, fear and limiting belief with reckless enthusiasm (as I did when I first learned how to clear), let's complete the ChapRecap before we take a look at the final step in the 1-2-3 clearing process: *verification.*

Chap-Recap #4

Food for Thought:
1. When you get clear, you get results.
2. There is no **one** true way. There are many paths to healing, many paths to clarity, and many paths to freedom.
3. Be still and know that you are God.
4. In healing yourself, you are beginning to change the world.
5. When we cut a cord, we cut all that no longer serves, with the intention that all the love, the fond memories, and everything positive remains.
6. Always cut cords from a place of love or at least, neutrality.
7. Some clearings happen almost instantaneously, while others take much longer. Be patient with yourself as you learn these new clearing techniques.

Action Plan:
1. Practice Praxis: Do a Cord-Cutting with someone or something you wish to be freed from.
2. Practice Praxis: Listen to the audio clearing referenced in this chapter.
3. Practice Praxis: Clear a block using a pendulum, or fashion a reasonable facsimile.

CHAPTER FIVE

Step 3. Verify It's Cleared, then Rinse and Repeat

The truth will set you free.
But first, it will probably make you nauseous.

~Amy Scott Grant

At this point, you're feeling good, aren't you? You've identified a pattern to release, you've discovered the root cause, you've cleared it, and now you're sitting pretty, right?

But how do you know it's really cleared?

What if you made this all up?

What if it's all just in your head?

What if it comes back?

What if it didn't take?

These are common questions so if you're wondering about any of the above, you are not alone. I'm going to show you some ways you can verify that your clearing is complete and whether or not it really worked.

Truth Testing: a process used to verify and/or validate

Truth Testing is a term I coined several years ago when I first began my own journey into energy work and self-healing. I needed an objective way to test for truth, otherwise the whole "energy thing" seemed too hokey and subjective for me.

Knowing how to properly perform Truth Testing is like having your own "easy button" for life. You can use Truth Testing to:

> Find out if someone is telling you the truth or lying. This works with anyone, but is especially helpful with kids and spouses. In my house, "It wasn't me!" has become a thing of the past because all I have to do is threaten to whip out a pendulum, and the culprit quickly 'fesses up.
> Make the best possible choices and decisions for yourself and anyone who asks for your advice. This works on everything from what to eat and what to wear to whether or not to take that job in Boston or divorce that cheatin' deadbeat…and everything in-between.
> Get your own second opinion when medical practitioners advise you to take this new drug or have that "routine" operation or stop eating red meat. You can also test any substance (including food, supplements, and meds) to determine how and to what degree it is likely to affect your body.
> And you can rely on Truth Testing to verify whether or not a clearing is complete.

There are countless ways you can use Truth Testing to make your life easier, but I'm only going to explain the basics so you can get started right now. This way, you'll know enough to be able to verify whether or not your fancy new clearing skills are working.

Besides which, you shouldn't have to take my word for anything—nor should you have to accept carte blanche anything a psychic, energy healer, or so-called "enlightened one" tells you. I'm a big proponent of self-reliance; this is why Truth Testing is the very first thing I teach anyone who wants to work with me.

It's necessary for you to know what's true so that you can decide for yourself whether or not the methods in this book actually work, and whether or not you really *can* heal yourself and others. (I mean, *I* know you can, but that's not nearly as valuable as *you* knowing you can. Capisce?)

There are many reliable Truth Testing methods, and in the spirit of this 1-2-3 guide, I'm going to share just three of them with you: the pendulum, the "body sway," and one that's likely familiar to you: the "gut check."

The Pendulum

The exact origin of the use of **pendulums** (also called *dowsing* or *divining*) in healing and energy work is unclear, although we know it has been used successfully for centuries. Water dowsing (a related practice) can be traced as far back as Herodotus the Greek in 5 B.C. When you think of a pendulum, your mind may conjure images of an old grandfather clock measuring the seconds with each swing, or perhaps you are reminded of hypnosis. Maybe you think of the song "Pendulum Swing" by the Indigo Girls. Whatever it has meant to you in the past, hang onto your socks because pendulums are about to get a whole lot more interesting.

A pendulum consists of a string or chain with an object of weight on one end. In a pinch, most anything can serve as a pendulum, and I've personally used nearby items such as a pendant on a necklace, a cell phone charger, a digital camera, a piece of yarn and a washer, even a water bottle. I'm not necessarily recommending any of these; I'm simply making the point that you don't need to buy anything elaborate to get started. If you prefer a fancy one, order yourself a special hand-made pendulum at www.custompendulums.com.

I'll take some time now to explain how to use a pendulum for Truth Testing and then in a later book, for healing. If you're more the visual type (or highly impatient) then just go to my website at www.InfoYesNo.com and watch the how-to videos.

The thing to remember is that there is no power in the pendulum other than the power you give to it. Can you see it for what it is? It's just a piece of string with a dangly bit on one end. The power comes from your Highest Self, the part of you that is connected to all of life and everything in the Universe. Truth Testing with a pendulum consists of three steps:

Step 1: Calibrate
Step 2: Phrase Your Question Mindfully
Step 3: Relax and Await Movement

Step 1: Calibrate.
Once you are experienced with using a pendulum, you can hold it any old way you want but if you're a newbie, start out the way I describe. This will help you to get your bearings and avoid any mixed signals. You might have noticed I like to set you up for success.

Sit up with your back straight and your feet uncrossed and flat on the ground. Pick up your pendulum with your dominant hand and bend comfortably at the wrist. Imagine the energy is coming off your hand and down into the pendulum, like a waterfall.

Keep your elbow down to keep your arm from getting tired. At first it can take a while until you get the hang of it and pick up speed. So for now, elbow down, and it's best while you're first learning to avoid resting your elbow on anything.

The dangly part of the pendulum should be even with the middle of your chest, so that your pendulum hangs about six to eight inches in front of your heart chakra. Relax your shoulder, your wrist, and your jaw. These are places where most people hold tension, and tension is just a form of resistance, and resistance is what stops you from being able to do energy work. Relax your jaw and this will remind you to release tension.

Remember, the pendulum can't do anything without a person, because the energy comes from the person, not the pendulum. If you have your shoulders scrunched up around your ears, how well do you think energy will flow through you? Relax. Breathe. Relax some more.

Now you can *calibrate,* to find out what your signs are. Calibration is fairly simple. You will ask three separate questions with a pause between each to check the direction of movement. It doesn't matter if your eyes are open or closed, but some people find it is easier to be patient when their eyes are closed as they wait for the pendulum to move. You can say these statements out loud or in your head:

Please show me a clear sign for "yes." Then wait for it to move and notice which way it's moving. If the direction is circular, notice whether it's clockwise or counter clockwise. Be patient and remain focused on the statement/question at hand, it can sometimes take several minutes if this is your first time. Once you make a note of your sign for yes, go on to the next calibration question.

Please show me a clear sign for "no." Again, wait for a clear and distinct movement, different from your sign for "yes."

Please show me a clear sign for "need more info." This will be your third and final sign.

For now, all you need to know is when you ask a question and your pendulum shows you the sign for "need more info" it's best for you to revise the question and ask again.

Step 2: Phrase Your Question Mindfully.
The quality of answer you get will be directly related to the quality of the question you ask. When you ask, be clear. Here are some suggestions for how to do that, and all of this is applicable no matter which Truth Testing method you are using.

Start with the phrase "all things considered." I recommend this phrase because it covers all bases, not just what you want, or what your brain thinks, or what your emotions are telling you in the moment. "All things considered" allows you to ask from a Divine perspective, across all time and space, transcending your mind and what is consciously known to you. It is all-encompassing, which means it produces a reliable answer based on a total 360-degree perspective (or perhaps 720 would be more accurate). It's like the difference between asking a question with a mere human brain, and asking a question as God. (Good thing I *never* exaggerate, right?) But seriously, it works, so start your questions with this phrase.

Next, you want to avoid language that implies judgment. Consider that in Divine Mind it's all good. Therefore, you may not get reliable answers if your question contains "judgy" words like "should," "can," "right/wrong," "good/bad," etc. Instead, stick with the highly effective yet neutral word, "optimal."

When mindfully crafting (not to be confused with minecrafting) your question, stick to what you can control right now. Truth Testing is perfect for making decisions and choices, and verifying whether something is true. "Is it optimal for me to call so-and-so?" is a far superior question to "Is so-and-so the right guy for me?" Likewise, "Is it optimal for me to submit my resume to XYZ Company?" is much better than "Is XYZ Company going to hire me?" Focus on what you can do right now, and ask questions that lead you to discover the best choice or decision in this moment.

Lastly, since you are looking for a yes/no answer, stick to just one variable per question. If you could only answer yes or no and someone asked you if you would like five thousand dollars that can be found inside an elephant's ass, you would probably be stumped. Not just because you're wondering where this person has been hanging out lately, but you could not answer if you wanted to say *yes* to five thousand dollars, but *no* to going head-first into an elephant's poop shoot. Whereas if you were asked, "Would you like five thousand dollars?" you could easily answer "yes" and then when asked if you'd like to fish it out of an elephant's rectum, you could (and hopefully, would) politely decline with "no." One variable at a time makes it easier to get a yes/no answer from your pendulum. If you get a "need more info" sign, it is likely that you sneaked in more than one variable without meaning to do so.

Here are some examples of well-phrased Truth Testing questions:

All things considered, is it optimal for me to have lunch with Julie?

All things considered, is it optimal for me to book my flight to Jamaica?

All things considered, is it optimal for me to hire Jackie for babysitting?

All things considered, is this meat optimal to eat? Alternatively, you could ask: all things considered is this meat safe to eat without risk of food poisoning?

All things considered, is Bertha (an employee) stealing from me?

Whereas, these are examples of poorly phrased questions:

Should I go out with Angela?

Is this the best job for me?

Is Fluffy the poodle going to die?

Is Santa Claus real?

Is Beverly drunk?

What's my phone number?

All things considered, does this pendulum make my butt look big?

Step 3: Relax and Await Movement.

This is the simplest, yet sometimes the most challenging part of using a pendulum. When you first begin, it may take several minutes before you see movement. It will get faster with practice. Stay focused on the question until the pendulum begins to move. Alternatively, you can distract yourself by clearly phrasing the question, then looking away for a bit. Think of Yoda perhaps. *Patience, young Jedi. Get answer you shall.* Then, when you see movement out of the corner of your eye, remove yourself from the Dagobah swamp and look at the pendulum for your answer.

Anyone can use a pendulum, even children. You can also test another person (or even an animal) by proxy, which can prove very useful in assessments and healing work.

The Body Sway

Body Sway is a phrase I made up. It's the equivalent of using your body as a pendulum and is very effective when you prefer a bit of discretion (not recommended while driving). Let's face it, it's not always convenient to whip out your pendulum during a corporate meeting or in the supermarket or in front of your ultra-judgmental mother-in-law. Or your veterinarian, perhaps. Or your gynecologist or proctologist. You get the idea. The body sway process is the same as the pendulum process.

Step 1: Calibrate.
Stand up straight with both feet planted firmly on the floor and your weight evenly distributed (in other words, don't lean to one side). Take a deep breath and let it out. While relaxed, ask for the first sign: *Please show me a clear sign for "yes."* Relax and see what you notice. Your body will do something. Whatever you feel or notice in your body is your own personal sign for "yes." Whenever you ask a question using Body Sway and you get that reaction, that's your yes.

Now return to that relaxed standing position and calibrate for the second statement: *Please show me a clear sign for "no."* Notice your body's reaction. Does your body do something different for "no"? Again, take note of this, as this will be your standard sign for "no."

Return once again to that relaxed stance and ask for the final sign: *Please show me a clear sign for "need more info."* What do you notice or what does your body do? This is your sign for "need more info."

What if you get the same sign for more than one answer? Easy, just recalibrate and this time alter your question slightly: *Please show me a clear sign for "yes,"* followed by *Please show me a **different** sign for "no,"* and then *Please show me a different, third sign for "need more info."*

I'd recommend that you stop reading here and try it yourself, and at the end of this explanation, I'll share the most common physical reactions to each sign. Otherwise, if I tell you now, you'll skeptically think it was the power of suggestion and that it wouldn't have happened if I hadn't told you it would. It's more fun to feel it, then read it, and think, "Holy smokes! That's exactly what happened!"

Step 2: Phrase Your Question Mindfully
See the Pendulum explanation above. You can ask your question aloud or in your mind. The main thing is just to be clear and specific, and don't include multiple variables (for example: is it optimal for me to wear the blue sweater with the red scarf and the black pants and the black shoes?) and don't ask for a prediction.

Step 3: Relax and Await Movement
You've got your signs, you've asked your question, and now you just relax until your body begins to sway or lean. Once it does, you've got your answer.

Easy, right? Take a minute to try it now if you haven't already done so.

As promised, here are the "standard" signs for the body sway. These are not absolute, and if you have different signs, don't sweat it (freak). No, I'm just teasing about the "freak" part. If you have unusual signs, you may find that over time, they normalize to these:

Yes = body sways forward
No = body sways backward
Need More Info = body remains still

The Gut Check

The **Gut Check** is exactly what it sounds like. But what's interesting is that we are not all built with a gut check. If you've ever heard someone say, "go with your gut" and you thought to yourself, "But what does that really mean?" then you might not be a person who can receive or rely on a gut response in making decisions. Instead, you might rely on your heart, how you feel about something, or you may need to speak to someone you perceive as an expert to get his or her input before you make a choice for yourself. The gut check is not for everyone, but most of us have it and not enough of us rely on it.

Before you have your next meal, ask yourself, "Is it time to eat?" and then notice what comes up. Do you hear/sense/feel your gut giving you an "uh-huh" or a "nah-ah"? Or does that yes or no answer seem as though it comes from someplace else? If you get answers from your gut, your best bet would be to start listening to it. It's like a muscle that gets stronger with practice, although sadly, there is no evidence that using your Gut Check will result in flatter abs.

As with anything in this book, you don't have to take my word for it. Try these methods out yourself and see what happens. Don't waste your time on something mundane, like "what is my telephone number?" Instead, try it out on practical, day-to-day decisions that you need to make. What to wear, what to eat, where to shop. That's where you can really see results and believe it or not, it's how your life can begin to shift for the better.

A Few Caveats about Truth Testing

Practice Makes Perfect. It would be unrealistic to expect that you would attain 100% accuracy right out of the gate. Any of these methods take practice (as with most things in life) in order to become proficient. The more you practice, the better you'll get, and the more reliable your responses will become.

Ask a Lame Question…Get a Lame Answer. Maybe there are no stupid questions, but there are definitely ways of asking questions that are less effective than others. For the best results, you want to stick to asking questions about the here and now (which, incidentally, is the only thing you actually have control over).

Skip the Predictions. In the in-depth book about Truth Testing, I'll explain in detail why predictions don't work. But for now, consider that the Universe is forever in flux, which means it's ineffective to use Truth Testing to ask prediction-type questions.

Put simply, a prediction that is true right now might not be true five minutes from now. If that's still confusing to you, research the Butterfly Effect or wait until my Truth Testing book is published and then buy it, read it, and become enlightened. Huzzah!

A Word about Bias. Yes, you can influence your Truth Testing method. I could write a whole chapter about identifying and eliminating bias, but for now just follow this simple rule: if you suspect you may be biased or you don't trust the answer you get, ask an objective third party to use truth testing to verify the answer for you. Don't tell them the question. That way you *know* it's an unbiased answer.

Other Ways to Know It's Working

Sometimes you don't even need to truth test because you can tell the clearing worked. This is often evidenced by the way you feel, which could manifest as:

- ➤ a *physical* change of some sort: that pain in your neck suddenly feels better; you yawn widely; you shiver; you feel like dancing or stretching or doing a fist pump.
- ➤ an *emotional* change of some kind: you cry and then want to laugh or sing; you feel a great weight has been lifted; when you think about the person or situation that was affecting you, you now feel "nothing," or completely neutral; you feel lighter or happier or freer; etc.
- ➤ a *mental* change of some sort: the monkey chatter in your brain has dialed down the volume or hit mute entirely; you are better able to focus and concentrate; you've stopped worrying about something that was causing you great stress up until the clearing; you now "think you can" and take steps in that direction; procrastination fades away; and so on.

Other times, you may see tangible evidence of the change, for example:

➢ Shortly after completing a clearing around money, someone who owes you money and has been out of communication calls you out of the blue or pays you back without a prompt from you.
➢ After a career or business clearing, new opportunities or clients quickly arrive.
➢ Soon after you perform a clearing around your relationship, your partner suddenly begins acting differently, to your amazement.
➢ You spontaneously drop a few pounds after a body clearing, or your clothing feels looser or you get a few compliments on your looks.
➢ After clearing your gluten sensitivity, you accidentally eat a cracker (or twenty) and have no adverse physical reaction whatsoever. Yippee!
➢ And other delightful synchronicities.

Now that you know how to test and see if your clearing is complete, you might be asking the million-dollar question:

What do I do if it's *not?*

Excellent question, dear seeker. Here are your options:

Option #1: Keep working on it.

There's no need to panic if you ask if it's cleared and get "no" as the answer. Simply ask more questions to find out what to do next. This is the order of questions I recommend:

➢ Is integration time required to complete the clearing?
➢ If yes, ask how much time is needed. If no, go on to the next question.
➢ What percentage is now cleared? You could check this methodically with a pendulum, as in "Is it greater than fifty

percent?" and then continue to ask in such fashion, narrowing down the range each time. Alternatively, you could just go with the first percentage number that pops into your head and then verify it with Truth Testing. That's what I do. But I'm also a gut-check person.

➤ What more is required to complete this clearing? This is an open-ended question that should reveal your next steps.

➤ Repeat the above until you get yes, the clearing is complete.

Keep in mind, sometimes the only additional action that's required is something simple, like a nap or a bath or a phone call. You might be asked to acquire a certain crystal, or write an intention, or take some action in the "direction of proof" of what you've just cleared. Whatever it is, the trick is to listen and go for it, instead of analyzing and second-guessing it. Easier said than done, by the way, at least until you build up your confidence in your clearing abilities and your trust in the Universe as well as your connection to it.

Option #2: Set it aside and let the answer come to you.

If you are the type of person who is patient and can surrender your desires and wait until the answer reveals itself to you, then this is a great option for you. Unfortunately, if you're anything like me, your friends may have a habit of saying things to you like, "Daaaaaaaang! Somebody forgot to take her patience pills today," in which case this option is not likely to work for you. Every time my bestie does a card reading for me, she bursts out laughing when she pulls the "Patience" card because she knows there will be eye-rolling and indignant huffs and puffs from me. Patience may be a virtue, but it ain't one of mine.

Option #3: Get outside help.

This is the done-for-you option, which I love. Don't get me wrong, I'm a fan of doing stuff myself, but sometimes you wind up spending more money and wasting more time and learning more stuff you didn't care to know when you try to fix the toilet yourself instead of calling in the professional plumber. Whether or not to hire a professional mentor or healer is really a personal preference decision, and it comes down to your priorities.

Do you want it cleared in the quickest possible manner?

Are you tired of working on it yourself?

Are you too close to the situation, or perhaps too attached to the outcome?

Do you have the desire and the cash, but not the time?

If you answered yes to any of the above, then it's time to get outside help. Luckily, I happen to know a few people I can recommend to help you clear dang near anything. Ahem. More about that later, wink wink.

Chap-Recap #5

Food for Thought:

1. There's value in learning Truth Testing because you can discern the truth, make better choices and decisions, verify third-party information, and determine whether or not a clearing is complete.

2. When you have a way to test for what's true, you don't have to take anyone's word for something—you can check for yourself to see if it's true.

3. There is no power in the pendulum (or any other healing tool) except for the power you give it. You are the powerhouse behind the pendulum, because it accesses information from your Highest Self.

4. Anyone can use a pendulum, even children, and you can use it by proxy to test for others and for animals.

5. When phrasing your question, the main thing is be clear and specific while avoiding predictions or multiple variables.

6. The quality of answer you get is directly related to the quality of the question. When you ask, be clear.

Action Plan:

1. Practice Praxis: Use the pendulum to experiment. Calibrate and take note of your signs. Make a few minor decisions (which shirt to wear, what to eat), and see what happens. Pay attention to the outcome and how you feel about it.

2. Practice Praxis: Experiment with the Body Sway. Start by calibrating, then use it to check in when making a few minor choices. Notice whether you prefer this method to the pendulum.

3. Are you equipped with the Gut Check? For the next twenty-four hours, pay attention to your belly area every time you are offered something (coffee, an invitation,

"would you like fries with that?") and see if you feel an "uh-huh" sense of yes in your gut or a "nah-ah" sense of no. If you feel it—even if it's ever so slight—keep working with it and exercise it, like a muscle. If you don't feel anything at all, then you probably weren't born with the Gut Check, so start paying attention to where you *do* feel answers when you are asked a question or offered a choice.

4. Using any of the Truth Testing methods (Pendulum, Body Sway, or Gut Check), check in to see if your clearing from Chap-Recap #4 is complete. If it's not, follow the steps in this chapter to complete the clearing.

CHAPTER SIX

Caveats to Consider about Clearing

You are an onion. But not so smelly.

~Amy Scott Grant

There are a few caveats to consider with this whole clearing concept.

Caveat #1: You can't mess with free will

As much as we'd sometimes like to, I have learned that free will is an absolute and you can't make someone act differently (although there are ways around that, but that's a different topic for another book). You can't "fix" someone who doesn't want fixing, and you can't release what you are unwilling on some—any—level to release. You can only change yourself, and only what you are willing to change.

God: "You can't mess with free will."

Bruce: "Can I ask why?"

God: "Yes, you can! That's the beauty of it!"

(From the movie "Bruce Almighty," starring Jim Carrey as Bruce Nolan and Morgan Freeman as God.)

Caveat #2: You are an onion (but not so smelly)

Consider that you are a complex individual, and any long-standing challenges you've had are multi-layered and multi-faceted. In other words, don't expect to do one or two clearings and suddenly find yourself holding the winning Powerball ticket. While it's true that clearings occur swiftly and dynamically, and rapid results occur more often than not, it's also true that the deeper the issue, the more clearing that's required to produce a dramatic result. Think of your internal belief network as an onion, comprised of layers upon layers upon layers. If you've got a longstanding issue with confidence, we may first need to clear your body issues or your financial issues or your childhood issues before we can get to that *bam-pow!* instant confidence you seek.

This type of multi-layered clearing is different from the repetitive cord-cutting and redundant clearing work that I dismissed earlier (with impatience and disdain). Here, we are not clearing the same issue more than once; we are clearing various facets of the issue. Sometimes when there is little emotional charge or attachment, we can take one clearing to resolve several minor, related issues. Other times, the issue was created in thick layers, and that's when multiple variants of clearings may be required.

How about an example for illustrative purposes?

Bobby has struggled with money his entire life, until he discovered clearing work. The first layer he cleared was related to his parents' beliefs about money, which were remarkably similar to his grandparents' beliefs about money. Bobby took responsibility for absorbing his parents' beliefs and making them his own.

Once he released this generational pattern, he was able to identify the next layer, which was related to a divorce from his youth. Bobby discovered that he was still blaming his ex-wife for the debt he carries today. He also found repressed feelings of regret and resentment, as he was mad at himself for foolishly rushing into marriage at such a young age. Once he released this and forgave himself and his ex, he began to feel differently about money.

He then realized that he had another layer to clear around money. This layer was related to feeling as though his personal value was related to his income. Bobby found this to be particularly eye-opening, as he began to see that the way he had used money up to this point was to make himself feel bigger, or stronger, or more successful, or to combat feelings of inadequacy when he compared himself to others. He began some deep healing work around his self-worth and learning to love and accept himself, and at this point, Bobby's money situation began to shift, but that was only the beginning. His entire life changed for the better, because now he was finally free to be happy as himself.

In hindsight, Bobby realized it was important to start by taking personal responsibility for his beliefs, and for his financial situation; then to heal the past with his ex; then to love and accept himself. These layers needed to come off in a certain order, not only to heal his finances, but to enrich his life and expand his awareness of himself. With each layer, he grew substantially. Had he simply started with the self-worth work, he would not have experienced the benefits of the release that accompanied his personal responsibility or the forgiveness work with himself and his ex.

By the way, in case you're wondering how to know which layers need to come off first, the answer is simple. It's the same way you know anything: ask for answers. More about that shortly.

A serious issue doesn't always require layers of clearing to shift. Here is an example of a real situation where one clearing changed everything.

My daughters bickered constantly. My husband and I were pulling our hair out over the constant upheaval in our household. We tried every disciplinary action and love-and-logic technique we could muster, but nothing worked for more than a day. We were at our wits' end. When I asked my mom friends about it, they all told me this was normal behavior for sisters who are so close in age. But I wasn't convinced. I saw the way my oldest turned into a different person when she was around her younger sister. She grew mean and spiteful. Soon her younger sister was beginning to model this behavior toward her little brother. Enough was enough. I wanted harmony in my house, and I was determined to get it, dammit!

I could not find the originating incident on my own (it's very hard for me to be objective when working on my own kids; more about that later), but I knew it was not from this lifetime. I called an intuitive friend and together we discovered the source and resolved it. A single forty-five minute session changed our family dynamic forever. I would not believe the difference in these girls' relationship if I had not seen it with my own eyes. Not only did the bickering disappear, but so much more arrived in its place! It is heartwarming to see these girls treat each other with love, affection, respect, and honor. I have not seen two sisters as close as these! Everything shifted because of one single clearing.

Many issues can be cleared with one powerful and pointed clearing, and it's delightful when this occurs. It would be lovely if all clearings were so swift and simple. But sometimes it is necessary for huge issues to come off in layers, either because there is something to gain from doing so (as was the case with Bobby), or because it would be a shock to your system to have everything shift overnight.

Everyone who's tried to lose weight would say they would love to wake up tomorrow at their ideal weight. But let's face it—there would be serious repercussions if that happened. If your goal is to shed forty pounds and you woke up tomorrow forty pounds lighter, your friends and family would worry. They might urge you to see a doctor or have your thyroid checked. You would be surrounded with fear and concern from everyone who knows you. Plus, nothing in your closet would fit. What would you wear to the store to buy new clothes? Can you afford to buy an entirely new wardrobe right now? You might freak out when you looked in the mirror. In fact, you might not even recognize your own face. Can you imagine how unsettling that would be, to look in the mirror and see a stranger staring back at you? You would probably get hounded by people who want to know your secret, or haters who think you're a fake. And I shudder to think about how badly your skin would sag!

Far better to release the weight over time, easily and without alarm. You naturally shop for new clothes, transitioning into smaller sizes. You smile when you look in the mirror, admiring the cumulative changes. Your skin has time to adjust and maintain its elasticity. Your friends smile and compliment, instead of frowning and whispering nervously. Can you imagine how much better this feels, inside and out?

Yes, as much as I love instant gratification (and who doesn't?) even I have to admit that *sometimes* it's better all-around when the major stuff comes off in layers.

After all, you didn't become fearful or wimpy or broke overnight—your current condition is the cumulative result of countless choices and decisions and beliefs, accumulated over time. We clear in layers, and you can't get to the inner depths (your deepest issues) until you've removed some of the outer layers. The good news is that you feel better, stronger and more powerful with every layer that's cleared, and most people begin to see results immediately. If you choose to do it yourself, have patience, Grasshopper. These things take time, especially if you are a novice.

In order to make the clearings permanent, it's optimal for your biggest issues to come off in layers. This requires patience and persistence, and it is why I do not personally perform one-off clearing sessions. I have no intention of opening a can of worms and then leaving you writhing in it. Ew. Rather, you tell me what end result you want, and I check in to ask how many sessions it will take, and if that is agreeable to you, we get to work.

Caveat #3: Fears, Phobias, and Addictions

These are deep-seated blocks and severe coping mechanisms which makes them particularly tricky to resolve on your own, and be forewarned—with regards to these, it sometimes gets worse before it gets better. If you don't want to open Pandora's box without a chaperone, I recommend hiring a professional like myself who is skilled in releasing phobias and addictions to help you with these humdingers.

Caveat #4: Resistance, Attachment and Bias

You are close to your problems. Too close. This gets tricky when you are trying to get a clear perspective, and yet you've got all this history and baggage. Add to that fire the desire for a speedy and specific outcome and you've got a recipe for frustration and bias. Plus, if you've got any resistance whatsoever, I can virtually guarantee you won't know it and it will result in sneaky self-sabotage. Many blocks and limiting beliefs can be cleared on your own, but sometimes you will find it takes too long or becomes too hard, and that's when you want to bring in outside help to move things along.

For example, it is very difficult for me to clear health issues for my own children, so I typically have to get help from another intuitive. As a mother, I am far too involved and too attached to an outcome. Their pain is my pain. Like most mothers, I just want to make it all better, immediately. Therefore, when one of my children is sick or hurting, I call my intuitive friend, who happens to be a former client. I trust her intuitive abilities, but I also trust her opinion as a mother of six children. Together in a clearing session, the two of us are able to find the root cause and resolve it.

Caveat #5: Obsess Much?

When we desperately want results and the energy around the solution is entrenched in need, this can result in obsession, which isn't good for anybody. If you are obsessed with clearing something, that is almost a sure sign that it's time to hire outside help. Your obsession is a cleverly disguised form of resistance (resisting what's true, right now) and it's going to keep you stuck and frustrated. Remember, you can't release what you aren't totally ready to release, and an expert healer can help you see clearly and address the remaining resistance. Let it go, Elsa. Let it go.

Caveat #6: You Do Not Need Fixing

This isn't as much a caveat as a word to the wise. Dear seeker, you are whole, complete and perfect. You do not need fixing. Please try to look at clearing work as a way to make your life better, to help you to be and do and have more of what you want. To fulfill your soul's purpose.

Avoid looking at clearing as a tool for fixing your jacked-up self. Because you're not. You're amazing. You're exquisite. Clearing isn't a nose job, it's a new perspective on your nose. It's releasing all the emotions around those bitches who made fun of it, and releasing the pain of all those stinging insults. Clearing gives you freedom from judgment from yourself and others. It doesn't change your nose (although it can), it changes the way you and everyone in the world sees your nose. Perfect, as is.

Caveat #7: Advanced Clearing

This is the kind of stuff I refer to as "trippy shit." For me, it's delightful work, but if you have little to no experience handling these types of situations, then it can become downright terrifying. I personally love clearing these advanced blocks, and am happy to help if you decide you'd like expert assistance with:

- Vows of silence
- Soul contracts/sacred contracts
- Negative entities, a form of energetic parasite with *you* as the unwitting host
- Portals and "haunted" spaces

> ➢ Identity clearings. These statements begin with the words "I am," as in "I am weak," or "I am less than." These are by far the most difficult to clear. I have developed a quick and powerful process for shifting identity beliefs and blocks, and it totally rocks.
> ➢ Deceased spirits who will not leave
> ➢ Ego work, very tricky for self-healing but I personally love it
> ➢ And other strange and bizarre blocks

Caveat #8: The Most Important Advice in this Entire Book

"Now that's what I call high quality H2O."

~Robert "Bobby" Boucher, Jr.
Portrayed by Adam Sandler in "The Waterboy"

I know, it sounds so simple that I shouldn't have to say it. But it's the most crucial thing for you to remember once you start performing clearing work. If you have any kind of adverse reaction after a clearing, you can bet it's because of dehydration.

Think of a clearing as an energy detox, and there is a physical, cellular detoxification process that accompanies it. No, I have no proof whatsoever. There is no science that I know of to back this up, except perhaps quantum physics and cellular memory. But I know this for a fact from the tens of thousands of individuals I have personally cleared: if people start doing clearing work (or have clearing work performed for them) and they don't remember to drink extra water, then they feel the physical symptoms.

Usually this appears as nausea, fatigue, lethargy, headaches, etc. If you have a big clearing, double your water intake for twenty-four hours. If you have a small clearing, drink two extra glasses of water that day. The more water you drink, the lower your chances of feeling any adverse physical reaction whatsoever.

If you're clearing for someone else, increase your water intake and advise him or her to do the same. If you have alcohol shortly after a clearing, drink extra water to offset the dehydrating effect of the booze.

Nope, coffee and soda don't count. No, it doesn't matter if you add ice or not. Just make the Waterboy's Mama proud and drink up. And stay away from that foosball, it's the deh-bil.

Lastly, in the interest of full disclosure, here are a few additional caveats to watch out for as you perform your own healing work:

You might have trouble receiving information intuitively.

You might stumble while trying to find the root cause.

There might be multiple root causes.

You might have challenges executing the clearing.

You might get confused or overwhelmed trying to figure out which method to use for a clearing.

You might not know what else needs to be done to complete the clearing.

It might look as though nothing has changed, even though you just removed a layer.

It could get worse before it gets better (typically only occurs with addictions, fears, and phobias).

You may feel stuck, like nothing works, or feel like a failure, especially if that's one of your blocks.

Your family, friends, and co-workers could make fun of you. (If they do, they totally suck.)

You might give up just before you break through and strike gold.

Other blocks could rise up in your space as soon as you get some stuff cleared. Those are the next layers, raising their hands in the air and saying, "Pick me! I'm next!"

You might get discouraged and want to quit.

But then again, any or all of these things could happen even if you don't do any clearing at all.

So isn't it worth it to at least try clearing and see what happens? If nothing changes you are no worse off than you were before. And if things do get a bit worse, that's probably what would have happened anyway, had you changed nothing.

If any of what I'm saying is true, if there's even a shred of possibility that this clearing stuff really works, think about all that you stand to gain from giving it a shot.

You owe it to yourself to see if this works for you.

Chap-Recap #6

Food for Thought:

1. You can't mess with free will.
2. The deeper the issue, the more clearing that's required to produce a dramatic result. Big clearings come off in layers.
3. When clearing fears, phobias and addictions, it sometimes gets worse before it gets better.
4. Many blocks and limiting beliefs can be cleared on your own, but sometimes you will find it takes too long or becomes too hard, and that's when you want to bring in outside help to move things along.
5. If you are obsessed with clearing something, that is almost a sure sign that it's time to hire outside help. Your obsession is a cleverly disguised form of resistance and it's going to keep you stuck and frustrated.
6. Look at clearing work as a way to make your life better, to help you to be and do and have more of what you want.
7. You don't need a nose job, or any other kind of "fixing."
8. After clearing for self or others, drink water, water, and more water…more than you think you could possibly need. The more water you drink, the lower your chances of having any adverse physical reaction whatsoever.
9. You owe it to yourself to test out this clearing stuff and see if it works for you.

Action Plan:

1. Write in your notebook or journal: What are you afraid could happen if you really jumped into this clearing work? Why is it worth the risk?
2. Practice Praxis: Continue working on some smaller clearings. Record your progress in a notebook or journal. If it helps, measure where you are when you begin a clearing (you could use a scale of one to ten) and then re-measure

after the clearing and record your results. For example, you might not like your neighbor, and on a scale of one to ten, you would rate this dislike fairly high, a six or seven. Then, after you complete a clearing around it, you might then rate your dislike for the neighbor as a four. This will help to show you the impact of your clearings, and to what degree the work is helping.

CHAPTER SEVEN

Done-for-You vs. DIY

*I hate to admit when I can't do something myself.
But when that happens, I'm immensely grateful to find
the right people who can do it and do it well.*

~Amy Scott Grant

You might be wondering if it really matters whether you do your own clearing or hire someone to help you with it. In the grand scheme, I'm a big fan of "whatever works," but it may help if you have an understanding of the pros and cons of each.

As you read through this chapter, you will notice that I have made every attempt to be honest and balanced throughout. This is the part of the book where the marketing gurus would advise me to try to push or sway you toward joining one of my programs or hiring me and my team to assist you. But that's not how I roll, so don't sweat it, I'll shoot ya straight.

There are clear and distinct pros and cons to each path, and I'll outline them here for you as fairly as I can. Certainly, there are advantages to hiring me or someone on my team, but I am not afraid to tell you that's not the only way to go. And let's face it, if you're in dire financial straits or you're on government assistance, it's not going to be easy for you to come up with the cash to hire any professional for this kind of work. In that situation, the DIY option may be your only possibility at this moment.

99

Regardless of which path you choose, it pays to be armed with information, so that you can make the most intelligent decision possible. Of course, the best way to choose is to check in and use Truth Testing. That way you know you're making the most optimal choice (all things considered). Now here we go:

DIY Pros

NOTE: I sometimes refer to DIY healing as "HIY," which stands for "Heal It Yourself."

You are in total control. Which means you can move as fast as you want to move, go in-depth where you want to, and skip over the stuff you don't want to deal with (but skipping can also be a con, see below.)

Privacy. It is always expected that mentors, coaches, and healers will use discretion with regards to protecting your privacy, but nonetheless, it can be intimidating to admit some of your deepest darkest fears and secrets to another human being. When you do your own healing, no one has to know anything you discover and your secrets stay safe.

Work at your own pace. When you hire a mentor or healer, that person is typically setting the pace, unless you are on a "pay as you go" route (which I personally do not recommend). Usually you would pre-pay a package and meet for sessions at regular intervals, but if you work at your own pace, you can speed up or slow down the pace of clearing, since you don't have to wait for your next session to get into another clearing.

Learn as you go. If you love to learn, then the DIY/HIY route can be fun as well as educational and productive. I am a life-long learner, so it seems only fitting that my journey began through my own learning and practicing on myself.

Learn so that you can help others. I personally would not be the masterful healer I am today if I had not endured the agonizingly slow self-healing trial-and-error process that ultimately led me to source my own methods and help countless others. If that is in your heart, then it is possible for you, too (or, if you want to go fast, you can hire someone to teach you how to heal yourself and others). I would not have gone the DIY route except that I was too piss-poor broke back then to hire anyone at all, much less someone who rocked at healing. Don't get me wrong, I am grateful for the path I took, but I am also abundantly grateful for all the money clearings I did to take me from broke to financially thriving.

Very low cost. In terms of dollars spent, the HIY/DIY path is going to be your most affordable. If you're especially resourceful, it can be free or practically free. Granted, it may take more time and effort, but if you love to learn, this will be mostly enjoyable for you. If you lack patience and are not a fan of learning new things through trial and error, then for you, the additional time and effort may not be worth the benefit of a lower financial expense. But if you're flat broke, you can start by doing it yourself and for Pete's sake, work on your money stuff so you can get yourself out of that hole and on to more prosperous pastures. Word.

DIY/HIY Cons

You are in total control. Which means it's a lot harder to recognize when resistance, bias, and self-sabotage are interfering with your progress. It also means if there's any chance of jacking the whole thing up, you would be the one doing the jacking.

Takes more time. Generally doing your own clearings will take longer, as you are very close to the subject matter and therefore, do not always have the most objective perspective. Likewise, you may lack the experiences of a professional healer or mentor, so you will naturally need more time until you have practiced and gained proficiency.

Sticky, icky, stuck. Working on yourself means things can and will get sticky, and sometimes you can get stuck in the ickiness of it all. This is in contrast to a mentor or guide who can keep you out of the soup by staying on track, reminding you not to sweat the small stuff, offering proven solutions, and sharing stories about themselves or other clients who have gone through the same thing you're experiencing.

You don't know what you don't know. Blind spots abound in self-healing, and sometimes you don't realize you're missing something important, or on a wild-goose chase, circling the same issue without ever identifying what's at the root of it. This is tricky, because you can feel as though you are making some progress, without ever getting to the clearing that will make the difference and cause the biggest shift.

Helping others is tentative at first. When you rock out a clearing that makes a huge difference for you, you may feel like you want to go out and repeat the process for everyone on earth. Noble as that may be, it could get you into a heap of trouble. For starters, just because one method worked on you, doesn't mean it will work for others. If you don't believe me, think about the fact that there are so many frickin' diet books on the market, many of which are bestsellers, and yet every day you could find someone who followed the method to a "T" and produced zero results. Everything doesn't work for every person, and clearing is no different. This is why I teach healers (including self-healers) to check in with the specific person, the specific circumstance, in that specific moment, and do what is optimal for that person, in that time, in that space. In order to get that good, you've got to practice on different people with different blocks and circumstances and over time. Between now and then, it can get a little hairy for you *and* the person you're trying to help.

It's all on you. Doing it yourself means little to no support, at least from anyone who's more experienced at this than you are. If you're a bit of a lone wolf like Chazz Michael Michaels and you prefer to go it alone, this isn't much of a con for you. Interestingly enough, when I first started on this path, I picked the DIY route because I needed it to be free, but later I also realized that I had a belief that said, "I can't rely on anyone except myself." Once I cleared that chunk of blocks, I was able to find and attract amazing mentors, workers, healers, services, supporters, and all sorts of talented individuals, which meant I never *had* to choose the DIY path again, unless I really wanted to. Again, this is a personal choice so pick the option that fits who you are and what you need.

Now let's dive into the pros and cons of the done-for-you option, which means finding a healer, mentor, or coach to work with you and clear your crap for you.

Done-for-You Clearing Pros

Pace can be quick. Not every healer moves as fast as I do, but people generally come to me because they want speedy results and that's what I provide. It also ensures that every session we have together is wildly productive. This is an advantage if you like to move quickly and if you like to get more done in less time. In nearly all cases, working with me is significantly faster than going it alone.

Clearings are quick and deep. Hiring a skilled professional (and I'm not the only one out there, by the way) means a swift identification and eradication of the root cause. There's no jacking around with figuring out what's going on and how to help. Any healer worth his or her salt will give you faster, deeper, more effective results than you could get on your own (unless you are already an experienced healer, in which case I'd be curious what drew you to choose this introductory guide book. No, I'm serious. Drop me a line and tell me.)

Results are proven. If you select a seasoned healer, it is fair to expect results. No healer is likely to guarantee results, because so much is dependent upon how willing you are to release the blocks that hold you back. However, it's reasonable to expect to see improvement if you show up and cooperate with the process to the best of your ability. This is not necessarily the case with self-healing.

The pressure is off of you. With the done-for-you option, you don't have to do it all yourself. You've got support, guidance, expert assistance, and a shoulder to lean on. The biggest frustration

I hear from those who do their own healing work is, "When I get stuck, I have no idea what to do to get un-stuck." Sound familiar? "I don't know how" is the main reason people choose the done-for-you option over the DIY path. If you've got enough pressure on you elsewhere in life and you don't need any more added to the pile, it makes sense to hire help.

It's fun! Generally speaking, clearing with an experienced mentor is exciting and fun. My clients tell me on many occasions how much they look forward to each and every session, and I can count on one hand the total number of times I've ever had a client no-show for a call. It's wonderful to have someone to share your wins and your breakthroughs, especially when that someone understands your deepest, darkest fears and secrets and is committed to you winning. Many of my private clients have become personal friends of mine, and a few have grown to become some of my very best friends. I don't take on new clients with the intention of gaining new friends, but having perfect clarity around my ideal client means that I naturally attract awesome people I enjoy being around.

Done-for-You Clearing Cons

Skeletons will exit the closet. Again, any reputable mentor or healer with an ounce of self-respect will go to great lengths to protect your privacy, but it's worth noting that you are taking a measured risk (of exposure) when you allow an intuitive to look and see what's going on inside of you.

It ain't cheap. Money is an exchange of energy and value, which means in most cases, you get what you pay for, and my rates reflect this. Of course, my team and I aren't the only healers on the planet, and there is a wide range of what you can expect to pay for healing work. But any healer who's effective, confident, gets results and trusts herself enough to step up to the task when you need help won't come cheap. Beware anyone who claims to be amazing at what they do and yet they want to help you for free or practically free.

It's usually prepaid. The most effective healers typically require prepayment, in a package or program format. I can't speak for my colleagues, but I can tell you why I do it this way. When I first became a mentor and healer, I charged a monthly rate. But somewhere around the two- or three-month mark, the client would hit a major block. At the time when they needed my guidance most, they would suddenly find themselves short on either time or money, and in tears, they would inform me that they had to stop our sessions. This was heartbreaking for them and for me! The whole reason I got into this line of work was to change people's lives, and now when they need my help more than ever, they have to walk away, stuck in the soup. As a mentor, this is the ultimate bummer. When I switched over to prepayment for a three-month minimum package, this problem disappeared entirely. Think about it: once you pay for something, you're in it, right? You will stick with it and get your money's worth. This prevents temporary changes in financial priorities and other forms of resistance taking over. Now that I've explained how this prepayment can actually work in your favor, let's be honest about the downside: you're coming up with a substantial chunk of change up-front, and there's no backing out once you're in it. Make no mistake, this is a significant investment in your life and your future. Sure, there may be less risky ways to "try before you buy" to make sure it's a good fit, but if you know this is the person to get you where you want to go, you've got to suck it up and lay down the cash to make it happen.

You gotta be open. Granted, this is true of either path you take, DIY or done-for-you, but it's especially true when working with an expert healer. If you're not ready to let it go, Jesus Christ himself can't make it go bye-bye. Why? Because free will reigns supreme. Nobody messes with free will (not even Jesus). Truly great healers will recognize resistance within you and offer solutions or clearings to help you open yourself up more, but you are wasting your money if you think you're going to "test out a healer and see what happens." To see any kind of dramatic shift, you've got to open your heart, open your mind, and be willing to get raw in order to get liberated.

This isn't therapy. As mentioned earlier, the pace can be very fast, and we tend to dwell on the clearing and what's available after the breakthrough, rather than letting you cry in your soup over the past. Yes, some sessions do become emotional, and when that happens, we roll with it and process it as quickly as we can before moving on to the clearing. But if you've been in therapy for a long time, and you love being able to just talk and vent and think out loud for an hour while the other person listens and validates and occasionally interjects, then this may not be a good option for you.

When you work with a gifted and masterful healer, many of your insights can actually arrive *between* sessions. I personally love this and I hold space for it to happen, because it means we get to be even more productive during the session itself. I can't speak for all healers, but there's no way in hell I'm going to let you pay me several hundred dollars per session just so you can kvetch about your life for an hour. People hire me for results, so yes, I'll let you bitch and moan for a couple of minutes, but then it's time to get to work so we can find out the source of this irritation and obliterate it. It's actually much more gentle than that, but I think you get the point. If it's therapy you want, go find a therapist. If it's clarity and results you want, then hire yourself a Spiritual Ass Kicker.

However you get there, clearing works, period. But please don't take my word for it. Read about some people who have put these methods into practice, and then do your own experiment. Test out the clearing process for yourself, and then connect with me and let me know how it went.

Here are a few testimonials from people who have put to use some of the free training from my blog and my websites:

* * *

106

"I listened to the clearing session on your site and popped onto everything of yours that you have sent me. I have not enrolled in anything of yours…as I am not currently able to. I have listened to you do some live clearings…and have been doing them myself on myself.

"Some amazing things have been happening. I developed some of my own clearing exercises around sexual abuse issues. They have been so empowering that I feel a significant shift within myself. It is actually helping more than almost anything I have ever done…including tons of reading…EFT…hypnosis…rapid eye therapy…and tons of talk therapy…etc. It's like these things just pop into my head. It is hard to even put into words how I am feeling…it is like I have this whole new world opened up to me that I thought I had to have someone else help me with. I can do it myself. I am feeling so much more connected."

~ Heather W.

* * *

"so cray cray, I just finished the [prosperity] meditation…husband texts…he got an almost 10K raise moments ago…saweeeet"

~ Audrey M.

* * *

"I have sat on this earth many a year seeing the true light beings who are fully embracing themselves in the loving heart way that they are and may I honestly say you my dear are the first who has given without expectation, without seeking or disempowering others. I truly am grateful to know that their are beings of 'Living Light' who are genuinely activated and open to give with the love of the light that rises within us all but many seem to not fully embrace in the way that I have come to see and know through my beautiful guides Ascended masters, Angels, and council of Living Light from whence I have come.

"I am deeply honoured and blessed to feel the genuine presence of your message through the heart that beams with light as yours truly does."

~ Simmone D.

* * *

"Amy, I want to thank you specifically for these clearing emails. They are helping me clear the crap out and helping get me realigned to understand my higher purpose."

~ Kristie G.

* * *

And here are some emails from real people who have worked directly with me and/or my team for clearing and mentoring:

* * *

"What can I say but OMG all good things must come to an end in order to move on to the next chapter? This has been, by far, THE most incredible growth in my life. I am so grateful to you and for you! Having welcomed you into my life has been nothing but good and amazing things. It is time to set your little baby bird free. Tough LOVE I know ;) You are such a giver and a lover and one hell of a clear confident mentor/teacher. Not only did I gain the most amazing mentor, I gained a lifetime friend! Thank you for all the validation and support and LOVE!"

~ Terry R.

* * *

"Thank you so much for all your help! I can't believe the amazing turns my life is taking from the work I am doing with your programs! Thank you so much for sharing your wisdom! Without you I would still be stuck toiling away at a failing business wondering if I would even be able to cash my paychecks! THANK YOU!"

~ Jennifer S.

* * *

"OMG, Amy! I can't even begin to tell you how grateful I am for having the chance to participate virtually to your retreat! The energy was OFF the charts! I totally loved it! Thank you, thank you, thank you for everything!

"The changes I create in my reality are ASTONISHING! I processed a lot during sleep and dreamtime and I still am. Thank you once more from the heart of my hearts for everything!"
~ Rene B.

* * *

"Wow Amy! Yesterday morning I paused and compared how I felt at the moment with how I would have felt 2 years ago…at rescue? All our work around "control freak" issues. My day yesterday would have been a complete disaster had I still had those issues lingering. Instead—I flowed!

"The evidence of our work together is obvious. I'm giving myself a HUGE pat on the back and if we lived closer I would barge on over and give you the BIGGEST hug ever!"
~ Diane A.

* * *

"A gal in the kitchen started talking to me…she's normally not exactly talkative. Had a nice yet short chat. Then another contractor that I work with popped by my cube just now. I noticed in the past that a bunch of them go to lunch together sometimes. Anyway she asked if she could buy me lunch if I would be interested in joining them for lunch when they go and they were planning to go today. Whaaaaaaat? The only difference is you clearing me! This is crazy cool!"
~ Julie H.

* * *

"Thank you Amy! I don't know what you did but I feel light as a feather! My mind is clearer, much better focus and energy and the anxiety is almost completely gone. I went through 4 liters of water in the last 12 hours too cos I was so thirsty and sweating bullets!"

~ Niki N.

* * *

"I just had to email you to let you know my fabulous news. You may not remember the types of clearing you did on me but the first one you did regarding my son and our separation. Well my dear… around the middle of last week, he asked his brother to see if I would give him my email address so that he could contact me. To make a long but lovely story short… since then, we have exchanged emails, made arrangements to meet and just last evening we had our meeting with lots of hugs and heartfelt exchanges.

"Amy, I believe that the clearing you did for me was instrumental in bringing it all about as it was extremely important for me at the time to 'be at peace' and allow him to find his way back 'home'.

"Bless you Amy and I am so grateful for the healing time we shared. I look forward to more in the near future."

~ Elaine M.

* * *

Chap-Recap #7

Food for Thought:

1. Checking in with your preferred Truth Testing method is the best way to know if you're better off choosing the DIY/HIY option or the done-for-you option. But regardless which path you choose, it pays to be armed with information so you'll go into it feeling prepared.
2. Pros to the DIY option include: total control, privacy, work at your own pace, learn as you go, learn so you can help others, and very low cost to get started.
3. DIY cons include: total control, takes more time, can get stuck (and stay stuck), you don't know what you don't know, helping others is tough without experience, and it's all on your shoulders (little to no support).
4. Done-for-you pros include: quicker pace, fast and deep clearings, proven results, pressure is off of you, and it's fun.
5. Cons of done-for-you are: skeletons come out of the closet, more expensive, prepayment is usually required, you must be open, and it's very different from therapy.

Action Plan:

Write down your answers to the following questions:

Which feels like a better fit for you right now, DIY/HIY or done-for-you?

If you picked DIY/HIY:

What kind of support will you need in order to ensure that you follow through with the clearing work? For example, quiet time in your home, designated time on your schedule, high-quality chocolate on-hand (optional, but recommended), a pendulum, a friend to verify if you have bias or resistance, etc.

What (if any) hesitation do you have around moving forward and doing your own clearing work? Do you have any fears or concerns?

If you chose the done-for-you option:

How soon do you want to find and hire a healer to assist you?

Do you have the funds on-hand? If not, brainstorm ten ways you could get the money (HINT: this simple exercise unlocks your mind around lack-thinking and begins to open you up to increased prosperity.) If you have the funds accessible, mentally earmark that money for this purpose.

What (if any) hesitation do you have around moving forward and hiring a healer? Do you have any fears or concerns? These are worth considering as you interview and/or research healer candidates.

Begin shopping for your ideal healer. If you'd like to work with me, you can learn more about my programs and packages at **www.AskAmyAnything.com.**

CHAPTER EIGHT

Your Next Steps

Nothing happens until something moves.
~Alfred Einstein

I make stuff move.
~Amy Scott Grant

Now that you know what to do and how to do it, and you know what your options are for moving forward, it's time to get that booty moving and take some action. Action is where it all happens, where it all comes together, and where miracles unfold. This is the precise reason there are "action items" in every ChapRecap in this book.

For the DIY/HIY Choice

Step 1: Make a list

Take some time to create a detailed list of what you would love to clear. What's in the way of you creating your most exquisite life? What would you love to be freed from in a year?

By taking the time to write out your answers to these questions in a notebook or journal, you are beginning to create them as real and lasting. Here are some journal prompts to get you started:

How would your life change as a result of releasing those blocks?

What's the payoff for sticking with the plan and moving forward on your clearing work, even when it gets tough and you want to quit?

What will you have to give up in order to shift away from where you are and into where you want to be?

What do you know about yourself with regards to handling adversity? In other words, do you tend to give up easily, get frustrated, cry, throw things, etc.? What safeguards can you put in place now to ensure that you persist beyond your typical responses when the going gets tough?

Who do you have on your side? Who supports you and lifts you up? Who can you trust with your hopes and dreams, without fear of jealousy or sabotage? Make a list of the people in your life you can count on to support you in your self-healing journey.

If your answer to the above question feels too short, take a minute now to set an intention for new support to come into your life, and make a list of characteristics of those supporters. What kinds of friends would you love to have in your life right now and how would you like those relationships to feel?

What are your strengths? What do you know you rock at? What do other people compliment you on?

How can these strengths serve you in your self-healing work?

What becomes possible if you can clear your own crap? What will be true for you? Who will you become?

What are your weaknesses? Do your best to answer this without judgment, but merely as an observation of fact. Knowing your weaknesses helps you to avoid wasting time on things you're not good at, and rather, seek out solutions that work. For example, I have no sense of direction and I frequently get lost while driving, even in my own town. Therefore, I always make sure that I have a

GPS to help me find my way, including in a rental car. Make a list of things you know you are not proficient in doing/handling.

Next, think of solutions and resources you can use to offset the areas where you do not excel. You may want to come back to this one. With time for it to percolate, more solutions will come to mind.

What have you always wanted to do, but haven't yet done?

What one thing from the list in the previous question would you love to do within the next ninety days? Write it out and assign a deadline to it using the power phrase "I will." For example, "I will go skydiving by [insert your deadline date] and I will rock it."

Anything else you'd like to express as you take this all-important first step toward self-healing? Write it down.

Step 2: Track your progress

It is well known that whatever we measure tends to improve, and healing is no exception. When I first started my own healing journey, I kept (and still have) spiral-bound notebooks. I used to write down all the limiting beliefs I wanted to clear, and then I would cross through each one and note the date I cleared it. That may be a little OCD for you, and that's fine. Record your progress in whatever way feels good and manageable to you.

Eventually, I learned to group related beliefs into power clearings, and then I would write down just the overall theme and cross it off the list once I had cleared that chunk of beliefs (sometimes in the thousands).

Later, once I had sourced newer, more efficient clearing methods, I kept a simple list of my areas of focus. As I performed clearings, I would check in periodically to rate my current status using this 1–10 scale.

10 = totally blocked; dense, dark blackness, heavy and oppressive; bordering on despair or hopelessness

9 = majorly blocked; rage or depression, extreme frustration, panic

8 = mostly blocked; agitation, anxiety, anger, sadness

7 = fairly blocked; disappointment, irritation, fear

6 = somewhat blocked; annoyance, impatience, lesser fear

5 = midpoint; confusion, doubt, tediousness; stopping here would likely cause a relapse

4 = blocked, but close to breaking through; hope on the horizon interrupted by bouts of doubt

3 = some blocks; not enough to stop me from manifesting or moving forward; feeling powerful

2 = remnants of blocks; have cleared enough to see results and begin to produce miracles; could stop here and all would be okay long-term

1 = nearly clear; only the slightest debris remains, what's left is barely noticeable

0 = no blocks; neutrality around the issue; freedom, liberation

Every few days, or after completing what felt like huge clearing work, I would go through the list and re-check it to see where there was evidence of progress. As I moved up the scale thanks to additional clearing, I would just cross through the old number and write in the new one. For example, while working on money, I might have started with clearing blocks around value and valuation; then moved on to money clichés, like "love of money is the root of all evil;" then advanced to blocks to accepting or receiving money; then moved on to clear blocks around debt. As each component within the bigger issue released, the bigger picture shifted as well. At this point, my tracking looked something like this:

Money = ~~10~~ ~~7~~ 4

Self-love = ~~3~~ 2

Patience = ~~9~~ ~~8~~ ~~7.5~~ ~~7.2~~ ~~7~~ ~~6.8~~ 6.5

Health = ~~6~~ 4

Trust = ~~10~~ ~~8~~ ~~7~~ ~~5~~ 2

You don't have to use any of these specific tracking methods, they are only described here to give you a few ideas of how it might be done. You could instead choose to simply rate how you feel each day on a scale of one to ten, or you might create your own tracking system entirely.

It is not essential to track your progress, but here's why I strongly recommend it:

As humans, we forget. We forget how low our lows are, especially when we feel high. We forget how much work we put into something to make it great. If you don't track your progress, you will inevitably reach a day when you are up against a huge block and you'll think, "What good is any of this clearing crap anyway? Nothing helps." That's the point when you'll want to quit, and many do, but please don't give up on yourself. You've come so far, and tracking will help you see that.

If you have proof that your life is improving... if you've kept a log of evidence that reminds your forgetful brain that your efforts are paying off and your clearing work really is making a difference, you will be more inclined to keep going when the going gets tough.

Many people give up on themselves. Tracking your progress is one simple way to avoid becoming a quitter.

Remember, your tracking doesn't have to be fancy or elaborate, it just needs to show you what's working and why you're pressing onward. That's all.

Do it. You'll thank me later.

Step 3: Keep growing and advancing

In my journey, I have learned that some of us are lifelong learners, and I know I am among these thirsty ones. If that sounds like you, I don't need to tell you to keep growing and advancing as your clearing progresses; you'll just naturally do it. I am where I am today because of my insatiable quest for learning and my desire to master the use of energy to positively impact lives across the globe (starting with my own).

What drives you? What makes you tick? What gets you excited, leaping out of bed to start the day? If you can link these core desires to your growth and advancement, progress will become automatic and you won't have to "make" yourself do it. Clearing will be a joy for you, as it is for me and countless others among us.

The best ways to grow are to read, to experience, and to experiment. This is why I offer amazing hands-on courses and programs like the HIY Fundamentals course, which is a prerequisite for the powerful HIY Mastery program.

If you enjoyed this book, stay tuned and grab some of my other books so that you can grow and expand and learn even more, discovering faster ways to clear your crap and liberate yourself. If this book isn't your cup of tea, look for healers and teachers who resonate with you. Get their books, their courses, and their programs. Learn all you can to keep growing and expanding.

If you're feeling a lack of support amongst your friends and family, you can connect with me on Facebook and ask to join my private online group, in order to meet other like-minded seekers. It's called Club Clarity and it's a great way to meet practice partners and expand your personal support network. Plus, this group is on my "first-to-know" list for special perks, new courses, and early-bird announcements, so if you like to be in the loop, that's one more reason to join us.

Visit my website www.AskAmyAnything.com where you'll find a ton of free and paid resources designed to help you expand and enhance your healing abilities.

Be patient with yourself as you grow and learn. Like any new skill, clearing takes practice, time and effort to master. Specifically, more than ten thousand focused hours is likely what it will take to become masterful at this. Give yourself the time and space to explore and expand as you feel your way into this new talent. Don't be afraid to fail; it's all part of the journey. Cut yourself some slack and remember to celebrate your wins (something we do a lot of in Club Clarity).

What if you get stuck?

If you hit a bump in the road, it helps to have someone else you can reach out to, to bounce around ideas. This is where it pays to have your support network in place. If you have little to no support currently, come and join us in Club Clarity and connect with some fresh faces and open hearts.

Hitting a block may also mean you've done all you can, and now it's time to get some expert help. In many cases, people hire me because they have reached an impasse with their own healing, or in working with another healer. I have a track record of succeeding where others fail, and together we blast through the tough blocks and create powerful breakthroughs.

The most important thing is not to panic. Stay calm—everyone hits a snag now and then, or comes up against a seemingly impossible block that just doesn't want to budge. Relax and put some space around it. If you can detach a bit, you'll be able to see what the next step is.

Next Steps For the Done-for-You Path

Step 1: Find the right partner for you

Naturally, I'd love for you to work with me. Unfortunately, I have a finite number of hours available for one-on-one work, which means the number of private clients I can accept is extremely limited. This is why I have personally trained a small group of spiritual leaders in my clearing methods, so that together we can help even more people who are ready to get clear. My Ripple Magic program is a group healing and mentoring format in which you work directly with my right-hand healers in private clearing sessions. Additionally, you get access to me through small-group intensive calls and retreats, all at a more affordable cost than working directly with me one-on-one as a private client. However, as I have mentioned previously, I am not the only person on the planet who is capable of powerful clearing work (thank goodness!) Of course, you may be hard-pressed to find another healer with my quirky sense of humor, my extensive memory bank of obscure movie lines, and my penchant for colorful language.

At any rate, it's important to find a partner with whom you resonate strongly, and who is congruent with what you need right now. With a growing market of energy specialists, alternative healers, Reiki masters, EFT practitioners, card readers, life coaches, and intuitive healers, you may feel a bit overwhelmed by your options.

Sometimes, you already know who you want to work with and have met/followed/been introduced to that person. Other times, you are on the hunt for your ideal healer or mentor. Here are a few helpful hints for finding the most optimal person for you, right now.

First, ask questions. Begin by asking yourself these clarifying questions to shed light on the kind of practitioner you'd most like to work with, and then make a list of questions to ask your potential candidates. Suggested questions worthy of your self-evaluation may include:

What do I need most right now?

On a scale of 1-10, how important is it to me that I get these issues resolved?

How quickly do I want to get these issues resolved?

Am I attached to a particular method of healing, or am I open to try anything? If a particular method is preferred, which one(s)?

What qualities would I strongly dislike in a healer? For example, perhaps you hate being rushed or pressured, maybe you have trouble understanding anyone with a thick accent, maybe you don't like the airy-fairy type, or perhaps you have a low tolerance for vagueness or ambiguity.

Based on the "dislike" qualities listed above, what is it that I really want? For example, if you can't stand vagueness, then you would want someone who is clear and direct.

You might think an obvious question would be "How much am I willing to invest in myself?" but that's not necessarily the case. It really comes down to what you want in a healer, and then when you find the right one for you, the money will come. I've never seen a truly committed person get stopped by something as mundane as *money.* Where there's a will, there's a way, which is only cliché because it's true.

Additionally, I tend to think it's a bad idea to limit yourself with a specific dollar amount. Whenever I've manifested my ideal living arrangements, I never attached a dollar amount (for example, "a house priced at or under $400,000.") What if the house that's really perfect for my family and me was priced at $402,000? Or worse yet, what if our ideal home was $300,000, and I wound up overpaying by $100k? Better to be clear about the features you want in a home, and let the Universe handle the cost.

Same goes for clearing work. Why limit yourself to someone who charges a certain amount for healing? Better to find your ideal healer and let the money sort itself out. Plus, when you find the person who truly resonates with you, what you gain from their assistance should far outweigh any dollar amount you've paid.

As I often say, you won't get what you want, you'll get what you ask for, so you'd better be damn sure you ask for exactly what you want.

Once you've explored the self-interview questions above, make a list of what matters most for your ideal healer. I call this your list of "must haves." Most of this information should be clear and easy to find by spending just a few minutes on the person's website.

NOTE: Beware any healer who doesn't list their package pricing or per-session rates in clear, easy to understand language and terms. I have never understood why some mentors, coaches, and healers want to keep their rates a secret. More than likely, they listened to some marketing guru who claimed people would be turned off by rates they perceive to be too high or too low. So… what happens? Do they arbitrarily choose a random dollar amount based on how the introductory conversation goes? Do they spend the intro call trying to convince the potential client they're worth it? It smacks of sneakiness and I personally don't trust a business that doesn't include their pricing (unless everything is custom, like art or floral arrangements). When I'm ready to buy, if I come across a site with no pricing, I leave and take my money and my patronage elsewhere. When it comes to mentors and healers, I would advise you to do the same.

Psychologically, a lack of clear pricing comes off as shady and underhanded. I also think sliding scales are a bullshit copout for the person who's setting the rates. If you're really that good, pick a rate and stand behind it. If you want to help the destitute, offer some pro bono work. But why would a coach disempower someone by affirming their broke-ness and adjusting their rate downward? The client won't be as committed, and the healer won't be as invested. But perhaps that's a rant for another day. For now, just know that if you are researching a healer and you can't find pricing or rates on their website, cross that one off your list and keep looking. *end rant*

Some general examples of questions to ask before you hire a healer might include:

➢ **Some measure of their experience.** For example, how long has this person been healing full-time? How many clients have they successfully helped, and to what degree? Have they worked with others in your situation or with your issues? You wouldn't want to hire a money coach to heal your marriage or your body. You also wouldn't want to hire a broke money coach, would you? Yet the sheer numbers of broke-ass "prosperity coaches" who are actively promoting their services would astound you.

➢ **What is the cost and what will you receive for that cost?** For example: number of sessions, frequency of sessions, whether or not email support included, are any courses or bonus material included, are there prerequisites, etc. Is there a payment plan (if you can't swing the full cost at once)? Is there a cash discount or other incentive if you enroll quickly and pay in full? I offer a "quick-start bonus" to anyone with the cojones to move forward quickly. The Universe loves speed, and so do I. I like to reward those who are decisive about what they want. You have nothing to lose by asking for a little something extra. Remember lagniappe?

➢ **What's the deal with their personal life?** I don't need to pry into someone's private life to know whether or not I want them mentoring me. However, it's important to me that anyone who's working on me at least has their shit together. I don't want a coach who's simultaneously undergoing divorce, foreclosure, and bankruptcy. The odds are slim that a person who attracted that much drama in their life at one time, could—while amidst crisis—remain clear enough to heal anyone else, so I'm not taking that risk.

But on the other hand, what about someone who is five years post-bankruptcy, has survived a bad divorce and a cancer scare, and now rocks their life with everything they've learned from their hardships? Sign me up! That person has life experience that no newly certified twenty-something-year-old life coach could hold a candle to. Before I work with someone as my healer or mentor, I'd like to know that *overall,* their life is working, they are happy, they're not a negative Nelly, and they are committed to working on themselves regularly. If they think they've "arrived" then they will likely have a God-complex or superiority issues and either of those would appear on my list of "dislikes" from the self-evaluation questions above. But hey, it's your life, so make your own choices. Just know that it's worth taking a peek at their personal Facebook page or other social media to see whether they slam people, complain constantly, whine about money, or otherwise have a shitstorm of drama in their life. Because that may not be the person you want to help you right now.

> **What happens after you sign up?** How does it work, what happens next, what do you do, what do I do, what do you need from me as a client, etc.? All are valid questions. I have an audio of a real client session on my website, so when people ask me, "how exactly does this work?" I can direct them to hear an example session to get a feel for how the session can flow. Because of this, I rarely get these kinds of questions; people generally just sign up and pay and we get started. But then again, my whole shtick is clarity, so would you want to hire me if my website was confusing or muddy or otherwise unclear? I think not, dear seeker.

As I mentioned, you should be able to find answers to all of the above somewhere on the person's website. What? They don't have a website, you say? Run—don't walk—away, fast as you can. In today's technology age, anybody can have a fully functional website up and running in less than three days. Even if they're building some fancy, elaborate, expensive website, they should at least have a temporary site for you to view, and not one that says "under construction." Seriously, the 1990s are well behind us. There's no such thing as a website that is "under construction" any more. Actually, a more accurate statement would be to say they are *all* under construction as websites are mainly dynamic and ever-changing works in progress. But regardless, if someone tells you they are a professional healer, yet they don't have a website, this is someone who is *not* serious about what they do. I would not recommend such a person. Not. At. All.

Once you've researched the general questions by looking at the healer's website, the rest of your questions will be related to your answers from the self-evaluation. Review your list of must-haves, and take a look at their presence online to see if this person feels like a match for you. For example, let's say this is your list of must-haves:

> Integrity
> Results-focused, effective

> ➢ Fun (a plus)
> ➢ Incorporates different healing modalities
> ➢ Speaks in plain English; direct, straight-forward approach

Okay, I admit it. That's a list that describes me perfectly. But it also describes the kind of person I'd love to work with, too. Your list may be very different. The main objective is to figure out what qualities resonate with you and then use that as a benchmark in finding your ideal healing partner.

I recommend starting with the person's online presence (website, social media, videos, etc.) Videos are ideal because you can see and hear what the person is like. If you want someone who's fun, it's a red flag if his or her video appears stiff and rehearsed. That's probably not going to be a good fit for you. Plus, videos show how *real* the person is. Some people are so obsessed with appearances that they edit out every little blunder, um, or uh, but I personally leave those in. I'm not perfect, and not afraid to admit it. I am a real person and I enjoy real people, so when you find me online, what you see is what you get. I don't like it when I get a sense of someone from their website, but then five seconds into a phone conversation, I'm wondering if I'm talking to their deadbeat cousin instead. Give me authenticity, dammit! But that's enough about me. Take a look at your list and look for evidence of your *congruency* with each healer you consider working with.

Also, take the time to read the testimonials, if there are any. Again, I would be leery of any healer who doesn't have any testimonials on their website. Anyone who's good at what they do will receive spontaneous, unsolicited thank-yous and breakthroughs from their clients. As you read these, look for the congruency within your list of requirements. Look for specific results, for authenticity, and balance in the reviews (in other words, they're not all five stars; there should be some that are "good" and "very good"). Remember to look for congruency with your personal list of must-haves.

Step 2: Take the leap

Seems rather obvious, doesn't it? I mean, why would anyone take the time to go through all of step one, discover what they want and need, and then find a person who actually matches that energy, and then *not* hire the person? Believe it or not, it happens all the time. Call it chickening out, call it resistance, call it lack-minded thinking or fear of the unknown, but it definitely happens. Don't chicken out. Once you find your ideal healer, pull the trigger and hire them immediately. Man up and git 'er done before you lose your nerve, and before she raises her rates due to increased demand.

If you need time to cobble the funds together, set yourself a deadline and decide that come hell or high water, you are moving forward.

This step is a true leap of faith. Remember that scene in "Temple of Doom"? Indiana Jones is petrified to take the leap of faith (okay, it was really more of a very large and awkward step than a leap). Beads of sweat drip down his face and the depth of the crevasse is dizzying; the updraft blows the book from his hands. But when he finally takes that deep breath and steps out into the vast unknown, he finds that his foot meets a solid path after all. The same is true for you. Yes, it's terrifying. Take the leap (giant step, whatever). It's worth it, *so* worth it in fact that once you do it, you'll kick yourself for all the time you wasted in putting it off.

Take the leap. Hire the healer. Then hang onto your socks.

Step 3: Don't settle for anything less than results

It is completely reasonable for you to expect results. It is not reasonable for you to expect *guaranteed* results.

Healers cannot and should not guarantee results. As much as we would love to, we can't and therefore we don't (and by "we," I mean the ones with at least a shred of integrity). I can promise to make a custom healing pendulum for you and ship it to you within a certain timeframe. I can promise that I will do everything in my power to release as much as we possibly can, as quickly as we can, in the time we have together. I can promise to give you my full healing power and focus during each session. But I cannot promise that you'll be ready to let go of everything that comes up. I cannot promise that *you* will show up and do the work. I can't promise that you'll be open and receptive and willing.

Besides which, there will always be the one jackass who want us to guarantee that they'll be rich within five minutes, or that their twenty-year addiction will magically disappear after session number one, or some other such nonsense.

This step is important because sometimes I talk to people who have hired healers and now they come to me because they didn't get what they needed from the others. But what's interesting is, they didn't necessarily speak up and tell the person they were dissatisfied.

Read the following story and think about which person you identify with most.

Here's the scenario: two people are out to dinner in a restaurant. Each diner places their order with the waitress and then turns their attention to the sparkling conversation. When the food arrives, neither person is satisfied with the dish they received.

One person says nothing, not wanting to make a fuss. "I'll just eat it. It's not that bad," this person thinks.

The other person calls the waiter over to the table and politely explains that the food is not satisfactory, and gives specific details. "I'm sorry, but I do not like this. The meat is very dry and the sauce seems very salty to me. Also, the vegetables are undercooked." The waiter offers to have the meal replaced and to make it right. The first diner says nothing, but quietly regrets not having the courage to ask for what they truly wanted. Alternatively, this person may secretly resent the other diner for doing what they themselves were unable to do.

Most people are like the first person. They don't speak up because they don't want to make a fuss or cause a scene, or they don't want to bother anyone. They don't want to appear ungrateful or difficult, and perhaps they are fearful that the waiter would retaliate somehow by spitting in their food or something equally as unthinkable.

But the second person actually gets what they want. And they did it without being rude or demanding or causing any kind of scene.

My husband and I went out to dinner with a group of friends recently. We all ordered, but when our entrees arrived, they were not up to par. Admittedly, we are food snobs. I grew up in New Orleans and have taken professional culinary classes, and we are hard-core Food Network addicts. The texture of the risotto was all wrong, and the scallops were under-seared and overcooked. We politely called the waitress over and when we quietly explained why we were dissatisfied, she offered to have the kitchen re-make our dishes. While the rest of our dinner companions exchanged comments that the food overall was "meh," we patiently waited and chatted with the group. We were the only ones at a table of ten who let the waitress know there was a problem, can you believe that? When our new dishes arrived, everything was executed perfectly. Really, what tastes better than impossibly creamy risotto topped with fresh scallops seared to perfection? Our meals were positively divine and we thanked the waitress and tipped her well. We left happy while the rest of the group left feeling dissatisfied.

What do you think happened in the kitchen that night?

Most people would assume that the chef was pretty pissed off but that is rarely the case in a well-staffed, reputable restaurant offering excellent food and service. In this kind of kitchen, the staff prides themselves on creating amazing food that makes their guests happy. When there is a problem, they go to great lengths to make things right.

The same is true of any healer worth her salt. If you express dissatisfaction with the service you're receiving, and you give specific examples (for example, I feel like we are spending a lot of time on my childhood, but I'd prefer to work on some past life issues) then it is completely reasonable for you to expect that healer to adjust their approach to give you what you want and need.

The average diner who has a bad experience will say nothing to restaurant staff, yet they will complain to ten friends and advise them against that establishment.

Most people will say nothing and walk away unhappy. Don't be that guy. That guy is a tool. Choose to be the better person, the one who kindly and firmly speaks up for what she wants, and expects to get it.

Whether it's a restaurant meal or a healing session, don't be afraid to ask for what you want. It's the only way you'll ever get it. And if you feel as though you can't, then add that to your list of crap to clear and move it to the top of the list.

> *It's a funny thing about life; if you refuse to accept anything but the best, you very often get it.*
>
> ~ W. Somerset Maugham

In Conclusion

You may have noticed I refer to this magnificent process as "clearing work," because it is work. I don't sugarcoat the truth for my kids, and I won't do it for you, either. It is fun work and surprising work and delightful work and mystifying work and enlightening work and deeply gratifying work, but make no mistake about it:

This. Is. Work.

I do not guarantee specific results, but I do make promises and I keep them. I promise that I will clear everything that you are ready to clear. I promise to be direct and honest with you in all of our dealings together. I promise to tell you the truth, just as I have done throughout this book. I promise to give you far more value than you've paid for. I promise to keep my ego out of our sessions. I promise that your life will change for the better. Because of this, and because of my rock solid commitment to the betterment of your life and your freedom, I am able to facilitate massive results and jaw-dropping miracles. I promise I will do everything in my power to create miraculous breakthroughs for you. But I cannot guarantee miracles. No healer can.

We do the work because the work is essential. We all benefit from the work. Sometimes the ways in which you benefit are unexpected. At times that makes you ecstatic, and at times it makes you irritated. But then we do more work and all is well in your world once again.

Clearing work is amazing. It will open your eyes, it will change your life. It will blow your mind, it will rock your socks.

But it can't do any of that until you do something. Get moving, take action, and I invite you to keep in touch and let me know if I can assist you in creating clarity and freedom from your blocks.

Liberation is totally underrated. Never underestimate the power of *clarity.*

Chap-Recap #8

Food for Thought:

1. Action is where it all happens, where it all comes together, and where miracles unfold.
2. It is well known that whatever we measure tends to improve, and healing is no exception.
3. Many people give up on themselves. Tracking your progress is one simple way to avoid quitting.
4. What drives you and makes you tick? If you can link your core desires to your growth and advancement, progress will become automatic and clearing will be a joy for you.
5. The best ways to grow are to read, to experience, and to experiment. Learn all you can to keep growing and expanding.
6. Hitting a block may mean you've done all that you can, and now it's time to get some expert help.
7. Find a healer you resonate with, who is congruent with your wants and needs. Get clear about what you want so that you can ask the right questions as you search for a healer or mentor.
8. Don't settle for a healer that's "within your budget." Be powerful. Figure out what you want and need, and then go find the money required to hire the right person. Better to hold out for the healer you really want than to save a few bucks and be disappointed in the results.
9. Remember, you won't get what you want, you'll get what you ask for, so you'd better be damn sure you ask for exactly what you want.
10. Beware any healer who doesn't list their package pricing or per-session rates in clear, easy to understand language and terms.
11. Once you find your ideal healer, pull the trigger and hire them immediately.

12. Whether it's a restaurant meal or a healing session, don't be afraid to ask for what you want. It's the only way you'll ever get it. And if you feel as though you can't, then add that to your list of crap to clear.
13. Never underestimate the power of clarity.

Action Plan:

Practice Praxis: Make a list of the first three blocks you'd love to clear. Prioritize them in order of importance or urgency. If you haven't already done so, take some time to write out your answers to the questions listed within this chapter.

Are you taking the DIY/HIY path?

Using the methods in this book, begin working on clearing the blocks you've listed in order of priority.

Keep track of your progress and make note of any insights or additional blocks that enter your awareness.

If you get stuck stay calm, and create some space around the issue. Take a break and let the next step come to you.

If you have little to no support currently, find me on Facebook and request to join my private Club Clarity. Set the intention to connect with fresh faces and open hearts, and to get the support you're looking for. Be willing to offer your support in exchange.

Have you chosen the done-for-you path?

Take your short list of potential healers/mentors from your ChapRecap #7 and review their web presence for congruency with what you want and need, as well as your list of must-haves.

If you can't find all the answers online, make a list of your remaining questions and contact the person directly. Ask your questions via email, or request a brief telephone or Skype call.

Once you are satisfied that you've found the right match for you, check in with your preferred Truth Testing method. All things considered, is it optimal for me to work with this person? Have at least one other person verify the answer, without telling them the question. This is important because if you have any fear or resistance (especially around spending the money), you may get a false negative.

Take the leap and hire that healer or mentor!

If you are not satisfied with the service, speak up and ask for what you want. Be clear specific.

Prepare for awesomeness!

Amy Scott Grant

THANK YOU

Thank for you taking the time to read this entire book. I hope you enjoyed the 1-2-3 strategy, as well as the exercises and anecdotes. Now you are armed with enough information to begin clearing your own crap. Go forth and get clear!

If you loved this book, please take a minute to write a quick review on Amazon or recommend the book via social media. Share your experiences with this book and invite others to check it out. This will assist others who've been looking for clarity in all the wrong places, so they can get the answers they seek to get clear.

Want more of the Spiritual Ass Kicker? Visit my online catalog at **www.AskAmyAnything.com/catalog**

Amy Scott Grant

BEFORE YOU GO... DIMMIT!

Meet my son Adam. Adorbs, right?

I had an epiphany when he was two and a half years old and he started saying "dimmit." He struggled to open his water bottle… "dimmit!" He dropped a toy… "dimmit!" When he couldn't get his shoe on properly ("dimmit!"), that's when I finally figured out what he was saying.

And I thought, DAMMIT!

I had stopped paying attention to something I need to pay attention to—in this case, watching what I say in front of my little two-legged mimic.

Luckily, my oopsie was easy enough to fix. The next morning, I taught him to say "shoot" and "rats!" and "bummer." I know, they're not nearly as colorful as the ones I prefer, but there's time enough for that later. He was still young, so he pronounced them as "shoot, ratsch, and bommer."

That's enough about Adam and me—**let's talk about YOU.**

➢ Are your oopsies easy enough to fix, or do some of them feel like colossal whoppers?
➢ Do you feel like you jacked up something important? Like a relationship. Or your career. Or your *life.*
➢ Think you missed out on a great opportunity?
➢ Does it seem like nothing is going your way, you're stuck, and it sucks?
➢ Or maybe you just feel like you lost your mojo, and nothing is moving forward for you right now.

If any of that sounds familiar, then you deserve a private session with me. We call this the "Get Your Mojo Back, Dimmit" session.

By the end of this phone call, here's what you will have:

➢ Complete clarity around where you went off-track and how to fix it fast
➢ A faster, easier way to move you forward than you ever thought possible
➢ A blueprint of the next steps to powerfully move you forward and get you un-stuck
➢ A great sense of clarity and relief, as though the smoke has cleared and now you can see what to do
➢ Peace with the past and enthusiasm about what's next

And, as a bonus, I'll help you identify the blocks that are still standing in your way, so you'll know what needs to be cleared to get what you really want.

My normal rate is over $500 per session. The Mojo session is a special deal (translation: deeply discounted for you, dear seeker).

To get the scoop and book your session now, visit **SpiritualAssKicker.com/mojo**

Are you ready to get un-stuck? Are you ready let go of the past and all the reasons you haven't yet? Are you ready to *Get Your Mojo Back, Dimmit?*

Grab one of the available spots now before they're all gone. Otherwise, you'll be the one saying "dimmit."

ABOUT THE AUTHOR

Thanks to her highly developed intuition and insatiable quest for human advancement, **Amy Scott Grant** has healed and helped tens of thousands of individuals in more than thirty countries through her speaking, writing, and mentoring. Her extraordinary gifts are peppered with a unique sense of humor and a healthy dose of levity.

In September 2013, Amy was inducted into the National Academy of Bestselling Authors and received a prestigious Quilly award at the Golden Gala Awards in Hollywood, California. She was selected as a Thought Leader of the Year Finalist in 2013.

Amy has created a number of successful courses and digital products, including Ripple Magic Mentoring, HIY (Heal It Yourself): Higher Power Tools, and MindTime™ meditations for kids at KidCentered.com. You can find Amy's writing all over the internet, as well as in the bestselling book *Inspired Marketing* by Dr. Joe Vitale and Craig Perrine; the acclaimed *Chicken Soup for the Soul: Life Lessons for Mastering the Law of Attraction;* the #2 bestseller *Change Agents* with Brian Tracy; and the *Spiritual Ass Kicker Series.* Amy's blog is a massive resource of original articles, resources and unique perspectives: **www.AmyScottGrant.com**

Connect with Amy and discover what's brewing on the horizon at **www.AskAmyAnything.com**

1-2-3 Clarity!

CPSIA information can be obtained
at www.ICGtesting.com
Printed in the USA
LVOW10s0355220517

535382LV00006B/597/P

9 780986 226908